ABOUT THE AUTHOR

NEAL SHOVER is Professor of Sociology at the University of Tennessee, Knoxville. In addition to his long-standing interest in the social psychology of crime, he is interested in organizational crime, the regulatory process, and the political economy of corrections. His *Constructing a Regulatory Bureaucracy*, coauthored with Donald Clelland and John Lynxwiler, will be published by SUNY-Albany Press in 1986.

AGING CRIMINALS

SOCIOLOGICAL OBSERVATIONS

Series Editor: **JOHN M. JOHNSON,** Arizona State University

"This series seeks its inspiration primarily from its subject matter and the nature of its observational setting. It draws on all academic disciplines and a wide variety of theoretical and methodological perspectives. The series has a commitment to substantive problems and issues and favors research and analysis which seek to blend actual observations of human actions in daily life with broader theoretical, comparative, and historical perspectives. SOCIOLOGICAL OBSERVATIONS aims to use all of our available intellectual resources to better understand all facets of human experience and the nature of our society."
—*John M. Johnson*

Volumes in this series:

1. **THE NUDE BEACH,** by Jack D. Douglas and Paul K. Rasmussen, with Carol Ann Flanagan
2. **SEEKING SPIRITUAL MEANING,** by Joseph Damrell
3. **THE SILENT COMMUNITY,** by Edward William Delph
4. **CROWDS AND RIOTS,** by Sam Wright
5. **THE MAD GENIUS CONTROVERSY,** by George Becker
6. **AMATEURS,** by Robert A. Stebbins
7. **CARETAKERS,** by David R. buckholdt and Jaber F. Gubrium
8. **HARD HATS,** by Jeffrey W. Riemer
9. **LOVE AND COMMITMENT,** by Gary Schwartz and Don Merten with Fran Behan and Allyne Rosenthal
10. **OUTSIDERS IN A HEARING WORLD,** by Paul C. Higgins
11. **MOMENTUM,** by Peter Adler
12. **WORLDS OF FRIENDSHIP,** by Robert R. Bell
13. **CHRONIC PAIN,** by Joseph A. Kotarba
14. **INVISIBLE LIVES,** by David R. Unruh
15. **SOCIAL ROLES,** by Louis A. Zurcher
16. **THE REHABILITATION DETECTIVES,** by Paul C. Higgins
17. **AGING CRIMINALS,** by Neal Shover

AGING CRIMINALS

NEAL SHOVER

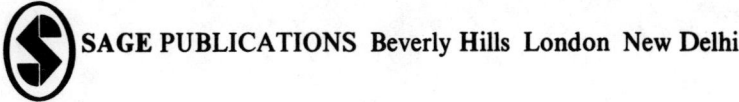
SAGE PUBLICATIONS Beverly Hills London New Delhi

Copyright © 1985 by Sage Publications, Inc.

All rights reserved. No part of this book may be reproduced or utilized in any form or by any means, electronic or mechanical, including photocopying, recording, or by any information storage and retrieval system, without permission in writing from the publisher.

For information address:

> SAGE Publications, Inc.
> 275 South Beverly Drive
> Beverly Hills, California 90212

SAGE Publications India Pvt. Ltd. SAGE Publications Ltd
M-32 Market 28 Banner Street
Greater Kailash I London EC1Y 8QE
New Delhi 110 048 India England

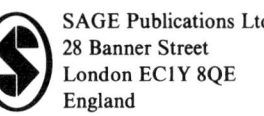

Printed in the United States of America

Library of Congress Cataloging in Publication Data

Shover, Neal.
   Aging criminals.

   (Sociological observations ; v. 17)
   Bibliography: p.
   Includes index.
   1. Crime and age—Case studies. 2. Aged offenders—United States—Case studies. 3. Recidivists—United States—Case studies. 4. Thieves—United States—Case studies. I. Title. II. Series: Sociological observations ; 17.
HV6163.S56 1985   364.3'7   85-14296
ISBN 0-8039-2528-X
ISBN 0-8039-2529-8 (pbk.)

FIRST PRINTING

AGING
CRIMINALS

Contents

Foreword	
by Daniel Glaser	11
Preface	15
1. Aging and Crime	19
What Does It Mean?	22
Methods and Analytic Approach	23
2. Illustrative Cases	29
The Uncommitted	29
The Unsuccessful	35
The Successful	46
A Look Ahead	54
3. Elapsing Time and Problems of Stigma	55
Daily Rounds and Situational Role Identities	57
Stigma Management	63
Persistent Offenders	70
Third-Party Disclosure	71
Stigma Disappearance?	75
4. Orientational and Interpersonal Changes	77
Specific Orientational Contingencies	80
Interpersonal Contingencies	92
Other Ordinary Property Offenders	97
Contingencies: Temporal Order and Interdependence	99
Perspective Change as Social Interaction	101
5. Changing Perceptual Controls and the Criminal Calculus	105
Negative Cases	117
Perceptual Controls and Differential Expectation	121

6. The Criminal Career and Related Experiences
   in Retrospect 127
      Retrospective Accounts and Regrets 128
      The Current Life 131
      The Prison Experience 139
      The Correctional Process 143
      Crime Partners and Acquaintances 147

Methodological Appendix 151

References 161

Index 171

About the Author 175

For their interest and kindness, this book is dedicated to the 50 men whose experiences are its base.

[The] potential to survive adversity, and even to thrive as a result of it, is one of man's greatest assets. Yet we know less about how people come to conquer hardship than we do about why they are overwhelmed by it. The concept of "recovery" has taken a back seat to the examination of "continued pathology." It is almost as though we have resigned ourselves to failure.

—Brown (1983: 188)

[S]o far as I can judge, present-day research into the problem of recidivism or "repeating" offenders tends to concentrate . . . a little too much on the subject of failure. This is . . . not hard to understand for sheerly practical reasons—because the failures, the ones who come back to prison, are of course the easiest specimens to study—they are available to be examined, diagnosed, analyzed, catalogued and categorized. But if the same sort of work could be done on the successes—on the people who, having had several convictions, had been in prison a number of times, manage at last as it were to put the brakes on and succeed in reintegrating themselves with society—how interesting it might be to try to find out just how they managed it, what sort of things helped them, what they found the most difficult problems to face, how they now look back on their successes and mistakes, and so on.

—An English convict
(Parker, 1967: 23)

Foreword

Crime has traditionally been viewed as a young person's detour in life's usual journey from "the lands of innocence" in childhood to law-abiding territories at some point in adulthood. It is people on this detour who commit most of the types of lawbreaking with which the police are primarily concerned. A majority of arrestees for auto theft, other theft, or burglary are teenagers, and these three offense categories constitute about 90% of what the FBI counts as Index Crimes, the types of acts that victimize others by which it charts the state of law and order in our country. Some of the perpetrators of these felonies soon end their meanderings on this detour into crime and return to "the pathways of righteousness," some go further on the detour, and some never depart from it.

We know that there is much greater diversity in the ages of termination of criminal careers than in the ages when criminal conduct begins. What makes lawbreaking stop, whenever it does? This is a neglected topic because it is difficult to study long stretches of lifetimes, especially those in which there are periods in the past that the subjects would like to hide. It is easiest to contact offenders when they are locked up so that we know where they are. They then usually welcome a chance to talk to someone, and this is when they are most often interviewed by social scientists. But when people are incarcerated, they can only speculate on if, how, and when their criminal activities will either cease or persist. Surely efforts to understand transitions from criminal to conforming behavior must be based on the study of persons who have made this change. However, to check on conclusions from research on such transitions one should also study as a comparison group the offenders who do not change—persons who started lawbreaking at about the same age as those who reformed, but who persisted in crime when the others ceased.

Neal Shover's book on *Aging Criminals* is one of the few that reports such research. It is probable that he is the first to study as many as 50 men, whose average age when interviewed was about 50, all of whom had been in prison but most of whom were then out, and most of whom started their seriously felonious conduct when teenagers or earlier—as is typical of our prison populations.

Shover's report is also distinctive because he tried to discern the relationships among types of thinking, varieties of feeling, and patterns of experience that might explain the behavior with which he is concerned, his dependent variable: the initiation or cessation of lawbreaking activities over the course of a lifetime. He makes a qualitative study of processes in conduct, rather than the typical quantitative enumeration of the small fraction of offenses that we are able to count and their correlation with other countable things. Those gains in understanding that behavioral scientists call *insight* on individual cases and *theoretical principles* when they apply them to categories of cases always begin in qualitative studies. Only after a qualitative conceptualization, if one can deduce from it some hypotheses about probable quantitative relationships, can statistical research possibly make its potential contribution to understanding, which is to strengthen or weaken confidence in the explanations that are evoked by qualitative conception.

Shover's study of aging criminals opens a new path to understanding why criminal conduct persists or ceases, because it reveals diverse patterns of change. We are sensitized by it to infer how the experiences of convicted felons affect their expectations of their futures in lawbreaking or in conformity.

We are given clues to these expectations by his descriptions of the ways in which his subjects experience and handle stigma, by their sense of success or failure in both criminal and legitimate occupations, and by their social relationships. Surely if we are to reform more criminals, or to protect society from those who are unlikely to be reformed, we must understand when, how, and why the expectations of prisoners and ex-prisoners change. Shover advances us in such understanding.

Today the most rapidly increasing age group in the population of the United States consists of persons over 85 years old. Increasingly, we are an aged people. Therefore, gerontology, the study of aging and the aged, is one of the fastest growing specialties in the behavioral sciences. Shover's book is a pioneering effort to fill a major gap in this specialty. It calls attention to a neglected aspect of aging, persistence or change in those personal standards of conduct that the law defines as criminal. It should thus interest specialists in gerontology as well as criminology within sociology and also persons with these specialties in other social sciences.

During the 1970s and 1980s there has been a burgeoning interest in longitudinal studies as the most fruitful method of gaining firm explanations for the dynamics of human behavior. In research on delinquency, crime, mental illness, and other conduct, a large proportion—perhaps a majority—of the landmark studies of this era have been longitudinal. I will not clutter this introduction with a list of all the books and articles that could appropriately be cited to confirm the validity of this assertion, but a few names and locations of some of the leading figures of this development may be informative: Donald J. West and David P. Farrington of Cambridge, England, Marvin E. Wolfgang and Joan McCord of Philadelphia, Lee N. Robins of St. Louis, and Sarnoff Mednick, who is simultaneously a professor in Los Angeles and a research agency director in Copenhagen. This very small sample from what could be a much longer list of authors in sociology, psychology, and psychiatry both illustrates the worldwide dimensions of the preoccupation with longitudinal studies and demonstrates its importance to anyone familiar with the deviance research literature in the behavioral sciences.

Shover's book on *Aging Criminals* is a new and important contribution to longitudinal study. It provides a foundation and a launching pad for anyone who wishes to project criminology further toward the understanding and reformation of convicted felons.

—Daniel Glaser
University of Southern California

Preface

To judge from the contents of most American criminology textbooks, everyone, students and teachers alike, wants to know about the causes of crime. Likewise, they want to know something of the road that leads from childhood to crime, from adolescence to the penitentiary. Obligingly—or so it seems—textbook authors unfailingly include materials on the etiology of crime and variations in criminal careers.

But there is a curious asymmetry in the conventional treatment of criminal careers. Although it is conventional wisdom that most offenders eventually desist from criminal behavior, criminology textbooks have little or nothing to say about this process. The later stages of criminal careers, whether this be transformation or eventual termination, have been slighted. It is time we begin to rectify this pattern of neglect. It is time we pay more attention to the later lives of the probationers, prisoners, and parolees who manage eventually to sever the links that previously tied them to the correctional apparatus. It is time we learn more about the ways offenders are marked by their criminal and correctional careers. This book is intended as a step in that direction.

The experiential origins of research projects are highly varied. Like the rivers and countless branches of the Appalachians, the sources of some are few and easy to identify; the origins of others can be numerous and impenetrable. Like those of the former type, the origins of this project are few and easily recalled. Some 20 years ago I worked as a prison sociologist at the Illinois State Penitentiary at Joliet. The file room there housed the records of all "active cases." It included a row of file cabinets containing the records of men under parole supervision. Several cabinets contained the "jackets" of absconders, men still on parole who had broken off regular contact with parole authorities. Although many of these men had absconded years earlier, the files contained no hint of their whereabouts and no evidence of subsequent contact with criminal justice agencies anywhere in the United States. For inexplicable reasons, I pondered the fate of these particular men. I especially wondered how they had managed to avoid the patterns established earlier in life. This research project is a continuation of that interest.

I incurred debts to and taxed the patience of many people in the course of this research. Patrick Langan prodded me to keep the project on a semblance of the planned schedule. More important, he took an interest in the research and provided useful bibliographic references that I might have overlooked otherwise. Officials in several federal and state agencies assisted me at numerous points in data collection. I especially appreciate the assistance of Stephen Reynolds (Administrative Office of the U.S. Courts), Harriet Lebowitz and Kathleen Tallis (Research Office of the Federal Bureau of Prisons), Jeff Ward (Maryland District Court), John Burkhead (Federal Correctional Institution, Lexington, KY), and Jim Pace, Bill Webb, Ed Muhlback, Paul Falconer, Dave Johnson, Carl Papa, Ed Linn, and John Calhoun (U.S. Probation Officers). Hildy Saizow, Jim Sulton, and Melvin Jackson assisted with data collection at various stages of the project. The man identified in Chapter 2 as "Jack Noble" consented to a lengthy interview and also helped arrange interviews with others.

Elizabeth Vodra, Kay King, and Letitea Johnson transcribed the interview tapes. They did an outstanding job, despite the problems posed by unfamiliar dialect and argot. Jan Jacobsen and Chris Link assisted at different stages of manuscript completion. Jeanie, Jenni, and Bubby (Douglas), my family, assisted me in many ways, not only with routine data management chores but also by overlooking a great deal of my absentminded behavior. Carole Haimelin expertly typed the manuscript and somehow remained cordial, despite the problems of working with me. Chris Link and Tony Miller offered helpful comments on several chapters. Jim (James G.) Fox, Chuck (Charles E.) Frazier, Don Gottfredson, and John Lynxwiler read and commented on an earlier draft of the manuscript. Their comments led to clear improvements in the manuscript, but I alone am responsible for any shortcomings that remain.

The opportunity and support required to complete the study were provided by a visiting fellowship at the National Institute of Justice. However, points of view or opinions expressed here do not necessarily reflect the official position or policies of the Department of Justice.

1

AGING AND CRIME

During World War II, the United States armed forces absorbed large numbers of males from the civilian labor force at the very time when the demand for industrial production increased. The nation faced a major labor supply shortage. To meet this need, thousands of American women took factory jobs and helped produce the armaments required for the war effort. American prisons were another source of badly needed manpower. Thousands of men were paroled to the military, thereby releasing other citizens for civilian work. Illinois is one state in which this policy was tried. During the years 1940 through 1947 the Illinois penitentiary system paroled a total of 2,942 men from its adult prisons who subsequently served in the Army. Most of these men were first offenders at the felony level, but many were recidivists (Lohman et al., n.d.).

After the war, as part of the Illinois Felon Study, a follow-up study of the military and civilian adjustment of these special parolees was conducted. During 1951-1953, a random sample of all the parolees inducted from the northern part of Illinois was selected, located, and contacted. Only a part of the results of this study were published (Reitzes, 1955; Mattick, 1960). Interviewed nearly 10 years after their release, many of these men presented a marked contrast to the persons described in their youthful correctional records.[1] As they aged, most of the men had foresaken criminal behavior and established conventional lives.

Given the well-known inverse relationship between age and criminal involvement, the decreasing criminal activities of these Illinois parolees is not surprising.[2] Hirschi and Gottfredson (1983: 552) call the inverse age-crime relationship one of the "brute facts of criminology" and claim that "no fact about crime is more widely accepted."[3]

It is not a recent discovery. As early as the mid-1800s, for example, the French statistician Quetelet (1969: 95) analyzed official crime statistics and concluded that "[a]ge (or the term of life) is undoubtedly the cause which operates with most energy in developing or subduing the propensity to crime." A century later, on the basis of their longitudinal studies, Sheldon and Eleanor Glueck likewise concluded that "[a]ging is the only factor which emerges as significant in the reformative process" (1937: 105, emphasis in the original).

Closer to the present, evidence from four sources supports and sheds additional light on the age-crime relationship. First, occasional ethnographic investigations (Glassner et al., 1983) and offender autobiographies show that many offenders either reduce or terminate their criminal behavior as they get older (e.g., Hapgood, 1903; Black, 1926; Clark and Eubank, 1927; Booth, 1929; Martin, 1952; Wilson, 1964; Edwards, 1972; Fletcher, 1972; King, 1972; Watson, 1976; Sopher, 1978; Jack-Roller and Snodgrass, 1982).

Second, analyses of aggregate arrest statistics show that the young disproportionately are arrested for, and presumably commit, more crime than older citizens (e.g., Sellin, 1958; Sagi and Wellford, 1968; Chilton and Spielberger, 1971; Greenberg, 1977).[4] According to the U.S. Department of Justice (1983:

31), 50% of all persons arrested for Index property crimes in the United States are age 19 or under. Comparable percentages for the 20-29 and 30 or older age groups are 31 and 19, respectively.

Third, self-report studies, in which individuals are asked to indicate how many times they have committed various types of crime, also show the inverse age-crime relationship. In their study of samples of three states, Rowe and Tittle (1977) found that the percentage of subjects who admitted stealing something worth $50 or more "during the last five years" decreased consistently from the 15-24 age group to the 65-93 age group. They found similar results for other types of offenses. Self-report research on known offenders has produced similar findings (Cline, 1980; Peterson and Braiker, 1980). For example, Petersilia et al. (1978) studied 49 California prison inmates, all convicted of armed robbery and serving at least their second prison term. Using a structured interview methodology, the men were asked about all the crimes they had committed, beginning with their juvenile years. Analysis of the data showed that "[t]he number of self-reported offenses committed per month of street time noticeably declined as the sample grew older" (1978: vii).

Fourth, the same age-crime relationship is evident in analyses of the arrest histories of known offenders (Farrington, 1979, 1983). For example, using its Computerized Criminal History File, the FBI examined the arrest records of 62,236 persons who were released from criminal justice custody anywhere in the United States during 1972. By 1975, 57.4% of the men had been rearrested at least once. However, the percentage of rearrested men decreased linearly from 64.4% of those who were under age 20 when released to 31.9% who were age 50 or older when released (FBI, 1975: 50).

The overall consistency of the evidence is impressive. Although there are some discrepant or ambiguous findings from a handful of studies (Blumstein et al., 1978; Blumstein and Cohen, 1982; Chaiken and Chaiken, 1982; Larkin and Greenberg, 1983), some elements of the age-crime picture seem clear. While Index property crime rates generally peak in the 15-21 age group and decline steadily with age, rates for some offenses peak at later ages than others or decline at a slower rate. Advancing age apparently leads to reduced involvement in Index property crimes, even by former officially processed offenders. Crime dropout rates are highest in the 18-early 20s age range, but a small percentage of Index property offenders persist in criminal behavior until their early 40s. Eventually, they too cease committing the types of crimes they committed when they were young. As they age, then, nearly all offenders with official juvenile records apparently desist from crime. On the whole, there seems to be sufficient empirical basis for the claim that the age-crime relationship is one of the "brute facts" of criminology. Clearly, something about advancing age produces reduced participation in ordinary property crime, even by those with extensive criminal records.

WHAT DOES IT MEAN?

A priori, statistical relationships such as the one between age and criminal involvement are subject to a variety of interpretations (Moberg, 1953). Consequently, we want to go beyond statistical description and explanation of this relationship; we also want to understand it experientially. Therefore, we must explore the human and social meanings of this statistical relationship.

The research reported here was undertaken to shed additional light on the later lives of men with official records as adults for ordinary property crimes, the changes they experience with aging, and the process of desistance from crime. In pursuit of these objectives, I resolved to identify, to locate, and to interview a group of men, now age 40 or older, who were involved in ordinary property crimes earlier in their lives.

METHODS AND ANALYTIC APPROACH

Materials

In collecting the materials for the study, I used both primary and secondary sources. Specifically, I (1) conducted personal interviews with 50 men who previously were convicted of and incarcerated for ordinary property crime; (2) examined arrest and correctional records for each interview respondent; (3) systematically examined autobiographies of comparable offenders, insofar as they include descriptions of the later phases of the authors' criminal careers; and (4) examined the transcripts from other interviews I have done over the past 15 years for comments about the process of desistance from crime.

In planning the study, I decided to limit the sample to men whose dominant pattern of criminality was ordinary property offenses such as burglary, robbery, auto theft, and grand larceny. Offenders whose criminal histories mainly involved forgery, interpersonal violence, or white-collar offenses were excluded. A variety of social science research suggests that offenders of the latter type may differ in important ways from ordinary property offenders (Lemert, 1953, 1958). By excluding them I was able to reduce the possible influence of confounding variables.

Offender Types

All the respondents were convicted at least once of ordinary property crime(s), but this superficial similarity masks a great deal of diversity among them. This diversity is not without limits, however. For more than a century now, criminologists have developed offender typologies in hopes of sorting out homogeneous groups of offenders. Although I neither desire nor intend to venture into this typological thicket, I found it necessary to distinguish the experience of subjects who differ in some important, fundamental respects. Earlier correctional employment, previous research (Shover, 1971, 1973), and familiarity with the offender autobiographical literature biased me in favor of employing an admittedly ad hoc typology. Nevertheless, the empirical merits of these research findings do not hinge upon either the elegance of the typology or its previously demonstrated value.

The typology was developed simply by cross-classifying two variables: *degree of criminal success* and *degree of identification with crime* as a means of livelihood. In the worlds of street criminals, the former usually is a function of the amount of money one has made stealing or hustling and the number of years one has spent in confinement (Shover, 1971). The latter cannot be described so easily. It means the degree to which one sees crime as an attractive and potentially lucrative source of income and livelihood. In the same way that some persons identify with and would like to become, say, doctors, others see crime as a desirable option (Glaser, 1956). As with aspiring doctors, however, not all those who would become competent, successful thieves or hustlers have equal opportunity to do so. They differ in native intelligence, ambition, and access to role models. Whereas some aspiring offenders exhibit intelligence and determination, and receive tutelage from established offenders, others prove unable to climb above the lower rungs of the occupational prestige ladder.

Each of these variables was dichotomized into high and low and then cross-classified. Bearing in mind the strictures already mentioned—all subjects were male, age 40 or older, and convicted primarily of ordinary property offenses such as burglary, robbery, or theft—the resulting typology includes

TABLE 1.1
Typology of Offenders

Degree of Criminal Success	Degree of Identification with Crime as a Means of Livelihood	
	High	Low
High	Successful a	b
Low	Unsuccessful c	Uncommitted d

uncommitted, unsuccessful, and *successful* offenders. Table 1.1 is a graphic depiction of the typology. Note that cell b consists of those offenders who achieve a high degree of success at crime even though they do not see it as a means of livelihood. It encompasses, presumably, white-collar offenders. Inasmuch as I did not include any offenders of this type in the research, they are not discussed here.

Uncommitted offenders score low on both the success and the criminal identification variables. Because few of them have any significant contact with older offenders, they rarely develop an appreciation for and identification with crime as an occupation. Their criminal involvement typically consists of one or a series of offenses. Their crimes are infrequent, poorly planned, and generally unremunerative. If arrested for their offenses, the arrest usually comes as a shock to those who know the offender, for it is seen as "out of character." They are the "square johns" and "lower-class men" sketched by Irwin (1970). Unless their crimes, in the eyes of criminal justice functionaries, have been particularly serious, uncommitted offenders often are placed on probation. They rarely are incarcerated more than once in their lives.

Unlike the uncommitted, unsuccessful offenders are those who see other offenders as positive role models and crime as a means of financial support. True, many of them vacillate about their choice, but at one time or another all entertain the thought that they can use crime as a means of livelihood. Whereas the uncommitted offenders commit very few crimes, the unsuccessful usually commit a much larger number. Due to a combination of personal and other shortcomings, however, their criminal exploits do not produce the financial returns— rarely more than a few hundred dollars—to sustain them for very long without the necessity to commit further crimes. Inevitably they are arrested and spend time in jail or prison. They correspond to the "disorganized criminals" and "state-raised youths" of Irwin's typology (1970).

As the name suggests, successful offenders are those who see crime as a means of livelihood and who do reasonably well at it. In their youth, most of them come into contact with older, skilled, and successful thieves or hustlers and they are attracted to the criminal life. The tutelage they receive from their older role models is extremely important in the development of their criminal skills. Eventually they approach crime as a vocational calling. Generally they commit many offenses during their criminal careers, and they may be incarcerated one or more times. Nevertheless, they spend less time in prison than the unsuccessful offenders. More important, their offenses are financially lucrative, often yielding thousands of dollars. They are the "thief" and the "hustler" in Irwin's typology (1970) of criminal identities.

Of the 50 interview subjects, I classified 9 as uncommitted, 36 as unsuccessful, and 5 as successful. Table A.1 (in the Appendix) presents some characteristics of the interview subjects. Most of the analysis that follows focuses on the unsuccessful offenders.

Career

Although the concept of criminal career is a staple in criminological textbooks, often it is not defined analytically.

As employed here, the concept of *career* refers to the typical experiences of individuals who have encountered, grappled with, and in some fashion resolved similar problems in their lives. The report examines only selected stages in the criminal careers of ordinary property offenders who were, additionally, largely unsuccessful in their criminal pursuits.

Careers have two related, although analytically distinct, sides (Stebbins, 1970). The *objective* career is open to public view and includes changes in lifestyles, social roles, and official positions. The *subjective* career is less visible. It includes changes in identity, self-concept, and the framework of imagery employed to judge oneself and others. Changes in both the objective and the subjective careers often occur together. Thus, to understand careers adequately, we must examine not only each of the two sides, but also how they fit together.

Career contingencies are significant occurrences, common to members of a social category, which produce movement along, or transformations of, career lines (Goffman, 1961: 133). Just as we can speak of objective and subjective careers, so too can we distinguish between objective and subjective career contingencies. The former are "objective facts of social structure" whereas the latter designate "change in the perspectives, motivations, and desires" of the individual (Becker, 1963: 24). In subsequent chapters I extract from the experiences of ordinary property offenders, and discuss typical patterns of age-related social psychological and behavioral change.

Although aging is used as the major explanatory variable in this book, I use it only for the sake of brevity and convenience. The biological process of aging is not the focus of attention; rather, it is the *socially constructed and negotiated changes in perspectives that accompany aging.*

NOTES

1. The source of these observations is Daniel Glaser. While employed as a sociologist-actuary at Joliet-Stateville penitentiaries, he conducted some of the interviews. He recalls the dramatic changes evidenced in the lives of some of the men he interviewed.

2. None of this is to deny that some older persons do commit crimes (Newman et al., 1984). Statistically, however, they account for very little *street crime*. Nor are these comments intended to obscure the fact that there are some older persons in American prisons. These older inmates generally fall into two distinct groups. One group consists of those, typically incarcerated for property offenses, who have previous criminal records. Members of the second group more often are confined for offenses against the person; unlike the first group, they typically do not have records of previous criminal involvement (Goettig, 1983; Langan and Greenfeld, 1983).

3. The label *crime* encompasses behaviors as diverse as rape, overtime parking, corporate price-fixing, armed robbery, and governmental violation of citizens' rights. Nevertheless, the mass media, agents of the state's crime control apparatus, and a significant proportion of the general public typically apply this label to a much more restricted range of such behaviors. They use it primarily to denote *street crime*, meaning offenses such as burglary, robbery, and auto theft. A substantial body of research literature suggests that most street crime is committed by youth or by young adults. Street crimes are committed infrequently by those under age 15 or by those over age 25.

4. Official crime statistics probably exaggerate the age differential in criminal involvement (Greenwood et al., 1980: 4-11). Still, few if any analysts deny that it is substantial.

2

ILLUSTRATIVE CASES

Here I present brief sketches of 7 of the interviewed men. The names are fictitious, and much of the material is drawn from official correctional reports. The men are typical of the theoretical categories presented in Chapter 1. Consequently, they are grouped into the same three categories outlined there.

THE UNCOMMITTED

Lonnie Eaton

Lonnie Eaton was born and reared in the Washington, D.C., area. When he was quite young, the parental home was broken by the parents' deaths. After that time he lived with various relatives, eventually spending most of his time with a sister and brother-in-law. Unfortunately, relations were not good between Lonnie and the brother-in-law. At the age of 16 Lonnie dropped out of school, and on his seventeenth birthday he enlisted in the Marine Corps. According to a presentence report completed several months later, he did so "because he didn't care to live with his brother-in-law any longer."

Lonnie was AWOL from his military duties on four occasions. During the fourth and final occasion, he went to a friend's home and, gradually over a period of days, the idea of committing crimes took shape. Lonnie remembered that his brother-in-law kept a pistol in his home. Lonnie took the pistol, intending to use it to commit crimes. Within one week, he and two other boys broke into several buildings, stole at least one automobile, and committed at least two armed robberies of gas stations and neighborhood grocery stores. Apprehended, Lonnie received a sentence of 2-12 years and was transferred to the Federal Reformatory at Chillicothe, Ohio.

The institutional classification report says of Lonnie Eaton: "Youthful in appearance, he has a pleasant manner and does not display any of the aggressiveness that one might expect from the nature of his offenses." Indeed, in the vernacular of correctors, Lonnie made an "excellent adjustment" during his confinement at Chillicothe. His entire period of incarceration was spent on a clerical assignment in federal penal industries and he maintained a clear conduct report. An institutional report prepared for the parole board three years after Lonnie began his sentence remarks that he

> has maintained above average work reports from the beginning. His supervisor states he has always found Eaton to be reliable and trustworthy in his work, and possessing a good wholesome attitude. . . . [He] is an excellent worker. In July 19--, he was named representative of his quarters to the 70th Inmate Advisory Council. . . . He has matured from an eighteen year old boy to a 21 year old man and is considered one of the best inmates of the institution by both staff and fellow inmates.

Lonnie was paroled after spending nearly four years in confinement, including nearly six months awaiting trial. When paroled, however, he was turned over to police in a D.C. suburb to face additional charges from the series of crimes that led to his incarceration. Lonnie appeared in court and the charges were dismissed.

> I can remember when [the judge] let me go. They said, "you've been released." And I walked all the way across that bridge from Arlington, Virginia home. I didn't even want a cab. It was raining like the dickens outside.... It didn't bother me at all. It was cold and it was raining but, boy, I'll tell you, it was the best thing in the world—to know that I could walk across there like that.

A day or so after receiving one of my letters, Lonnie called me and I explained the research project to him. We met at my office on a Saturday morning to do the interview. While he proved to be a helpful, interesting subject, he was extremely nervous. On the recording of the interview, one can easily hear the distinct smack-like noises he made as he tried to moisten his lips and mouth. He is one of only three persons in the sample who has never told another person about his experiences of arrest, conviction, and confinement.

Now 45 years old, Lonnie has worked over 20 years at the same skilled trade: the installation and repair of industrial equipment. He began this work only a few months after parole and, except for changing employers once, he has pursued it since that time. There were occasions when he feared his criminal record would become known; at least twice he underwent a security check as part of his work. However, no one ever indicated knowledge of anything unusual about his application or background.

Shortly after his release from Chillicothe, Lonnie looked up an old girlfriend. They began dating, and married a few months later. Although four children were born in rather rapid succession, the marriage was not a good one and there was much conflict. This was the focus of many comments in the parole officer's reports during the nearly 9 years that Lonnie was under supervision. By the time he was discharged from parole, the parole officer's report indicated some improvement in the marriage. It notes further,

> The subject has gotten along excellently. He has a good job, is buying his home, has not been arrested, and generally is making a fine adjustment. . . . [H]e is friendly and cooperative. The chances of his, again, being arrested are minimal.

The parole officer's prediction proved correct. Lonnie's rap sheet shows no arrests since his release from Chillicothe more than 25 years ago. When interviewed he was in the midst of a divorce, and he indicated that his wife once had him arrested—he spent one night in jail—on a charge of nonsupport. The likelihood that Lonnie ever again will be involved in any serious criminality seems extremely remote.

Wesley Barnett

The youngest of six children, Wesley Barnett was born in the rural South to a family of sharecroppers. The family moved to Washington, D.C., when Wesley was 11 years old. The father, a heavy drinker, separated from the mother the following year. According to Wesley's correctional records, the father later was convicted of homicide and incarcerated in the penitentiary. Following the parents' separation, one of Wesley's brothers was convicted of robbery and served a sentence in a state penitentiary. Another brother—perhaps the same one, the records are unclear—subsequently was incarcerated in a federal reformatory. Correctional records indicate that Wesley only attended school through the third grade and dropped out at age 16. He spent a portion of his school years in a special program for children considered retarded. (Subsequent testing at Chillicothe indicated he was of borderline intelligence.) At age 12 Wesley was placed on probation for the theft of a bicycle, but he had no other juvenile record.

His first marriage occurred when he was 18 years old. He and his wife eventually had two children. Although Wesley maintained steady employment, the marriage was stormy and he apparently spent much of his time "running around and drinking" with one of his brothers. At age 20 he and another man, after spending an evening in several bars, assaulted a man on the street and took his wallet. They were arrested a few days later, and Wesley spent nearly one year in the D.C. Jail, awaiting disposition of his case. Convicted, he was sentenced to 2-6 years, which he served at Chillicothe.

Wesley spent approximately 2 years at Chillicothe and worked in the chair factory the entire time. A report written just prior to his parole notes that he maintained a clear conduct record and received "outstanding reports" on his work assignment. It states further that

> [Wesley] has been consistently well behaved, mixes with a mature group, and is very considerate of others. He has always been cooperative and willing, has needed only a minimum of supervision, and has always made a careful, conscientious effort to do a good job.

He attended evening academic classes and was described as a "quiet, pleasant person who [takes] interest in his work."

Paroled, Wesley returned to D.C. to find, by his account, his wife pregnant. Regardless, he moved back in with her and their two children. The relationship was conflict-ridden, and Wesley's responses to the conflict apparently were rather simple, if indeed not primitive. On one occasion he and his wife quarreled over her use of the telephone. As he describes the incident today,

> I called the phone company up and told them to come and [take out the phone] and they said they'd be down there in a half-

hour, 45 minutes. I waited that long, I waited about an hour, hour and a half, two hours. They never did come. So I took it and snatched it out of the wall, threw it out the window.

On another occasion he reacted to marital conflict by leaving home. He temporarily moved to another city, and it was not until later that he considered the possible repercussions for his status as a parolee—he failed to secure permission to move. Eventually, after contacting his parole officer and returning to D.C., the parole officer placed him in jail for several days. The parole officer decided to continue his parole and Wesley decided his marriage could not be salvaged. He moved out on his own.

Throughout his term on parole and continuing for several years thereafter Wesley worked as a counterman and short-order cook in a small restaurant. The records indicate that he was a steady, dependable worker. He maintained this line of employment until he began construction work some 16 years ago.

I found Wesley's name in the telephone directory and called him. He readily consented to talk with me. He and his second wife, and their 17-year-old son, live in the apartment where I interviewed him. Wesley proved to be a rather simple, unreflective respondent, one who answers questions quickly and with little elaboration.

Several weeks before the interview, Wesley's driver's license was revoked for 30 days after he refused to take a breathalyzer test following a minor traffic accident. Besides the license revocation, he was cited for driving while impaired. He was hopeful his license would be returned the following day. He also said that in a separate incident earlier he was cited for driving while intoxicated. From this and some of his other comments it seems apparent that he spends a substantial portion of his leisure time drinking and socializing in bars and taverns. He has tatoos on both arms and on his back, all of which he acquired during his stay at Chillicothe.

Except for worrying about his first wife and children, his two years of incarceration were not difficult. He gambled and engaged in some petty hustles and, although he is not afraid of confinement, he sees it as a waste of time and a severe deprivation. He has learned that "the only way you can get anything honest is to work for it. Ain't nobody gonna give you nothing for nothing, you know."

THE UNSUCCESSFUL

Robert Timmons

An only child, Robert Timmons was reared by his mother, whose regular employment left him with little supervision. As he tells it today, "my mother didn't have too much control over me because I ran in the streets. I was a street child, really.... I was in the streets most of the time." Robert first came to the attention of officials at the age of 9, charged with being incorrigible. A report from that time states that he is "constantly truant from school, stays out late, lies, and steals." Released on probation, Robert was placed in a boarding home. However, because of misconduct and running away, he later was committed to the D.C. Industrial Home School at Blue Plains, Virginia.

Robert was before the juvenile court again at 13 for taking a bicycle (placed on probation) and at age 15 for housebreaking (again placed on probation). When he appeared in court again at age 15, charged with unlawful entry and escape from the detention home, Robert was committed to the Bureau of Prisons' National Training School for Boys (NTS).

After three escapes—during one of them he was charged with assaulting a woman with an iron bar—and while not yet 17 years old, Robert was transferred to Chillicothe. He remained there for two years before returning to NTS and a parole two months later.

Less than two months after his release from NTS, Robert was convicted of attempted housebreaking and received a 60-days sentence. Released, less than one year later he was sentenced to 6-18 months on a charge of assault with a deadly weapon. Within a few weeks of his release, Robert was convicted on multiple charges of carrying a deadly weapon, unlawful entry, and larceny. He received combined sentences of 15 months. Less than one year later, he was convicted of robbery and received concurrent sentences of 1-3 years and 2-7 years. He began this sentence at the D.C. Reformatory at Lorton, Virginia. After a knife fight with another convict and the loss of 200 days of "good time," Robert was transferred to the U.S. Penitentiary at Atlanta, Georgia. He was discharged via conditional release after serving nearly six years. Six months after release from Atlanta, Robert and another man were arrested and later convicted on multiple charges of armed robbery. They had robbed a cleaners but were arrested shortly after making their getaway. Robert received a total sentence of 9-27 years, which he began at Atlanta.

Robert has been a Muslim for many years, and openly acknowledged this during his various periods of incarceration. Along with his apparent inability or refusal to kowtow to correctional personnel, his religious beliefs and his insistence on practicing them openly probably added substantially to the problems he encountered from the correctional establishment. As he says today, "See, now, I was defiant. And for a black person to be defiant in an institution, he's asking for trouble." During his stay at Atlanta, Robert was accused of proselytizing and with holding a "cult meeting" on the prison yard. After one year at Atlanta he was recommended for transfer to the federal penitentiary at Alcatraz Island, California. The report that recommended transfer charges that "he is a rabid racial agitator and is constantly trying to stir up trouble in that connection." Further, it claims that "he is a definite menace to the morale and good order of the institution." Convinced of his dangerousness, the Bureau of Prisons transferred Robert Timmons to Alcatraz, where he remained for more than 8 years.

Today, Robert states that when transferred to Alcatraz he believed he never would be released alive from confinement. This belief only served to reinforce his resistance:

> I was really defiant, even to the warden, and I said, if I have to die, I'm gonna die just like I am. [I] said, nobody's gonna change me.

As good as his word, Robert must have been a nuisance to the prison officials at Alcatraz. Although he did not receive many misconduct reports, included among those he did receive were reports for fighting, fighting in the dining room, insolence, and refusal to obey orders.

Robert did, however, acquire some experience at a variety of work assignments while there, and eventually worked as a barber. He continued to practice his religion—a report notes that he was "very faithful" to it—and was seen by the prison staff as "race conscious." Despite the ominous tones of the official reports, Robert states that he began to change himself while at Alcatraz.

In the early 1960s, when the Bureau of Prisons closed Alcatraz, Robert was transferred to Atlanta. Today he states that the transfer made him feel "fantastic" and "for the first time I felt free." Nevertheless, he remained there for another 6 years. During this time he continued the process of self-change that began during his days at Alcatraz. Robert's final release from confinement occurred nearly 14 years ago. He was arrested approximately one year after release, but the charges were dismissed. This was his last contact with the criminal justice system.

The contrast between the Robert Timmons described in his correctional records and the man I interviewed is substantial. I found him to be pleasant, almost ebullient, and interested in my research. Now nearly 60 years old, he has been employed for the past 13 years as a hospital technician. He says that he enjoys his work, and this is confirmed by the way he talks about it. There is nothing about him or his demeanor to suggest that he was largely "state-raised" and has spent nearly half of his life in correctional institutions.

Although Robert married after his final release from prison, he is separated from his wife at the present time and lives in an apartment in a Washington, D.C., suburb. He berates himself for what he regards as an excessive personal indebtedness, but otherwise expresses happiness and contentment with his present life. He no longer is active in Islam because his fondness for women conflicts with its teachings and he doesn't want to be a "hypocrite."

Until several years ago, Robert believed he had no living relatives. However, when his mother died he was contacted by a woman who told him she was his aunt. Through her he learned that he also has several step-siblings. The discovery of these family ties has a great deal of meaning for Robert now. He visits his family often, and obviously enjoys the warmth of these contacts. As yet none of his relatives know about his prison record, but he plans someday to tell about it. As he puts it, "I would like them to know that I haven't always been the nice person I am today."

Carl Horton

A rather passive, quiet man in his mid-50s, Carl Horton was on federal mandatory release when I interviewed him. When asked how many calendar years he has spent in confinement, he responded, like the vast majority of the interview subjects, "I haven't figured it up." Like the others, he could only estimate: "I kind of guess, I think maybe about 17 years." (Although it is impossible to determine with precision from examining his rap sheet, this sum seems too high.)

Carl is the youngest of five children, and his parents separated when he was approximately 12 years old. Carl remained with his father for a year, and then joined his mother and siblings, who since had migrated to D.C. There was very little family cohesion and Carl, being the youngest, was left to fend for himself. Although he apparently was free of official involvement in delinquency, he began drinking heavily by age 21, a habit he has maintained his entire life.

Carl was first incarcerated at age 19, when he served six months for robbery. As he describes the incident today:

> I was drinking in an alley with some people, and this guy supposedly had been robbed. Or something like that. And they locked me and this girl—Mary something, I can't think of her name—concerning it. He claimed he was robbed of, I don't know how much money, but I didn't have a penny on me, nothing. And it wind up where they broke it down to a misdemeanor.... Anyway, I entered a plea and they gave me six months.

While incarcerated he "met people and got to know guys in there." He was fascinated and captivated by their accounts of criminal activities:

> I listened to them talk about how to make money, big money.... And I got to thinking I was kinda' smart then. Tryin' to figure ways to make money illegally, you know, without working too hard for it.
>
> Q: You wanted to be a good hustler, huh?
> A: I wanted to, yes.

Carl never realized his criminal ambitions because "I figure I didn't have the intelligence or something, the know-how or whatever. . . . I never had any luck."

Carl attributes nearly all his criminality to the combined effects of momentary need for money and the influence of alcohol. He says that when pressured for cash and intoxicated, he is easily led and also tends to do "stupid" things. Carl never has robbed anyone, and estimates that he has committed no more than 10 burglaries in his entire life. They were unskilled and yielded little return; he notes that he never made more than $200 from any of the crimes committed.

Carl once worked for nearly 4 years as a baker, but it has been many years since he last held steady employment. Today he has few occupational and social resources from which he can draw. He never married but did father a child by a girlfriend some years ago. He has no contact with either of them today. His siblings live in another city but, so long as his fortunes are down, Carl avoids contact with them, primarily because of the embarrassment it would cause him.

Carl believes that he wasted many years of his life and, indeed, he tends to speak about it in the past tense:

> I had dreams of doing better for myself, and making life better for myself, you know. I had dreams. And I kept dreaming and dreaming and dreaming, but they never quite came true.

Today Carl appears overwhelmed by the downward turns his life has taken. Most of his youthful dreams, both legitimate and illegitimate, have vanished. Although he is dissatisfied with his present life, he knows that his advancing age makes it unlikely that he will be able to secure work and a steady income. Asked to describe a typical day, Mr. Horton said,

> Well, I get up about 5:30. I shave and wash up. I come out and if my friend, William, don't have any jobs, I go down to, go catch the bus to Georgia and Alaska—that's the District line—and stand around and wait for somebody to dig footings, or pour

concrete, or something like that. . . . And I would stay there until about 9:30. If I don't catch out [get day labor] by 9:30, I hitchhike a ride back downtown. If I got money, I catch the bus. But if I don't have money, I'd hitchhike a ride. And I come downtown and stop around two or three places where the guys hang around. They drinkin' wine and stuff like that. Somebody always got something. We drink some wine or, you know, whatever. And if I got anything at home, I go home and eat me a sandwich or something like that. If not, I'll go around to one of these places where they give away free food. They got about 3 or 4 places around here where you can go and all you have to do is line up and go in and eat. . . . That keeps you holdin' together, in physical condition, you know. That's about it.

Ray Jackson

Carl Horton and Robert Timmons are clear examples of men who did not succeed at crime; they realized minimal economic returns, yet spent many years in prison. Ray Jackson is similar to them, with one difference: He continues his criminal pursuits and clings to the belief that he yet can acquire sufficient monetary returns to reverse the pattern of his earlier years at crime. It is too early to know whether his high hopes will be realized, but his record thus far indicates clearly that he belongs with other men who have been unsuccessful at crime.

Although he is in his early 40s, Ray Jackson has been convicted of felonies on four different occasions and has spent approximately 17 years in prison. Referred to me by another subject, I interviewed him at his home. He was on parole at the time, having been released from the penitentiary several months earlier. I was able to secure very few official records on Ray, so most of what I learned about him and his background was gleaned from the interview.

Ray was born in Baltimore and reared in a small, intact family. His first arrest, at age 11, was for burglary, which resulted in probation. Three years later he was arrested for auto theft and sentenced to the state training school, where he remained for nine months. After nearly one year on parole, Ray was recommitted to the training school. He ran away less than two weeks later. Arrested in another state, Ray was convicted of auto theft and sentenced to three years. He was three months short of his eighteenth birthday when he began his sentence in the state reformatory and he served the entire sentence.

Correctional records indicate that Ray experienced many problems. In the reformatory he was involved in several fights with other convicts, was implicated or suspected of stealing from other convicts, and generally displayed "aggressive tactics." Correctional officials charged that he had a "hostile and resentful attitude" and "constantly displayed contempt for the regulations and routine." After a few months in the reformatory he was transferred to the state penitentiary. His behavior showed little change in the penitentiary setting, and he was tagged as a "paranoid schizophrenic." After a few months he was transferred to the state's institution for the criminally insane.

Today, Ray states that because of his age and youthful appearance he was subjected to sexual pressures from other convicts in the reformatory. Predictably, these problems persisted—if indeed they did not intensify—in the penitentiary setting.

> I was only eighteen *then*. And I was way too young for that institution. And, yeah, there was so much pressure on me there. I think I just, well, I *did* lose it; there was no doubt about it. Then I went to the [unit for the insane], I spent, all the time I was there I spent locked up.

Nevertheless, "hospital" records indicate that he was involved in an incident described as a "mutiny" and "riot," during which he was in "possession of dangerous instrumentalities." He is described as a "very dangerous, assaultive, and paranoid schizophrenic" who "has been involved in assaultive behavior and has shown a persistent pattern of hostility."

Looking back at this first period of felony confinement, Ray says that it "was a hell of an experience for me" and "they really put it on me." He became extremely bitter about the treatment he received from justice and correctional officials during his initial term of imprisonment. He harbors little bitterness toward the other prisoners who preyed upon him during this time.

> I was more pissed at authorities for putting me in a position where I would go through all that shit.... That's not only doing three years, that's putting me through a lot of torment besides.

Released at age 20, Ray returned to his mother's home. Today, however, he says that when he "got out of that [institution] I wasn't really prepared to live anywhere else, other than a penitentiary. They really put a trip on me."

After a few months in the free world Ray was arrested on a charge of assault and battery. Convicted, he served six months in the county jail. A few days after his release he was arrested for burglary and unarmed robbery. He was convicted of these charges—and also of a charge of attempted jail breaking—and sentenced to the state penitentiary. He served nearly six years before his parole. After less than two weeks in the free world he was arrested on a charge of armed robbery and returned to the penitentiary, remaining there for an additional six years. Paroled again, Ray remained in the free world for nearly five years before he was arrested for burglary and safe cracking. Sentenced to 2-10 years, he was paroled after a year and a half, several months before I interviewed him.

Ray says that he did not get along well during his early prison terms and spent much of his time in "the hole." Later this pattern changed:

> 'Course, after awhile, you know, I was in there so many years I finally began to—I learned how to manipulate the system, you know. And, like when I went back this last time, you know, when I went in, I got the right cell block, the right job, you know. I manipulated the system to work for me. But most guys

don't know how to do that. But it took me years to learn that, too.... Like this last ten years or so I done, it was real easy time.... I didn't do that much of it in the hole or anything. I didn't have that hard of a time.

He completed many educational programs while in the penitentiary and later was an instructor in a vocational program.

During the early years of his second lengthy prison sentence (six years) Ray resolved to turn away from future crime and try to make it by working. However, he remained in the penitentiary for several more years and became increasingly pessimistic about his chances of succeeding at legitimate work. Nevertheless, when released on parole, he felt that he "wanted to get a job and work for a living." Once again, however, he says he was ill prepared for life in the free world:

> I got released from a maximum security institution. And the whole line of thinking in one of them institutions . . . is altogether different than what it would be in the world, the free world. And my thinking was geared to that penitentiary. And . . . it took me a long time to sort of get my feet on the ground. . . . I was far too violent, for one thing. And people were uneasy around me, and it showed, you know. I was just too violent, and I probably brought a lot of that penitentiary paranoia out with me. So it seemed like the only people I could relate to . . . were other ex-convicts who'd done a lot of time, like I had. . . . At that time I didn't really feel like I had a whole lot to talk to [other people about]. I personally had never been out of the penitentiary enough.

Ray made some effort to work, but supported himself primarily by "petty hustles" he learned in the penitentiary. After one year on the streets he decided to devote his time and energies to becoming a thief.

Ray had a "good name" from his years in prison and also had established contacts with some men who were skilled thieves, primarily burglars. He began stealing with them. He states that the financial returns from their burglaries were high and he lived well during more than five years of freedom, his longest period of uninterrupted freedom since age 15. His good fortune ended with arrest, and he was sentenced to 2-10 years.

Ray views his earlier criminality as nothing more than "getting into *trouble*" and he contrasts this with the crimes he committed in later years, during his five-year period of freedom:

> I started stealing when I was a kid.... [T]he trouble I got into, I was really never after no financial gain. I was just, it was more of a delinquent problem than I was trying to achieve anything. I never really decided that I wanted to steal anything for profit until I was about 35.... [A]ll the time I did prior to this last sentence, you know, I never made no money at all.... If I'd have got away with the things I *did* I wouldn't have made no money.... Now I know that's [stealing] what I want to do.... I just don't want to hurt no one. I don't want to do anything violent to hurt anyone.... But I'm going to steal.

Today Ray intends to resume his criminal pursuits. He says that he has weighed the potential gains and losses carefully and concluded that he has little to lose by returning to theft. He wants to be a "good thief." I asked him why this is his ambition.

> Well, at this stage of my life I think that's the only thing left open to me, that I can really profit from. I'm not going to be successful working. I don't want to work. I don't want that day-to-day grind and I don't want that regimentation that goes along with working a job.

So long as his crimes are nonviolent he risks, in the event of arrest, prison sentences of no more than 18 months. He is optimistic and confident.

Ray doesn't "want to take no unnecessary chances," but says that he is "going to try to make some money":

> [A]ll the experiences, all the things I've learned over the years, the people I've met—mainly the people I've met—just sort of finally gelled for me, you know. We're not talking about stealing no $300 or $400 or something. We're talking about,

we're talking about pretty big money, you know. . . . I'm interested in stealing as long as the money's right. I'm not interested in stealing just to be stealing. I'm just strictly interested in the money. If it's profitable, I'll do it. And I think what I know, and the people I know, can be profitable now. . . . I *can* make money from stealing. The chances of me getting busted are pretty slim, you know. . . . I know the odds are on my side, as far as getting away with a crime.

Ray indicates, however, that he only has a few more years to devote to stealing—"another six or eight years, or something like that"—before he gets too old to continue. He intends to steal until age catches up with him, his skills become obsolete, or the threatened penalties are raised to a point at which he is unwilling to gamble his future.

THE SUCCESSFUL

Jack Noble

Today, Jack Noble is nearly 70 years of age and lives with his second wife in a quiet, older suburban neighborhood near Baltimore. Their two grown children live nearby and visit often. His wife purchased the house during Jack's final term of incarceration, and few if any of his neighbors know much about his background or reputation. But, when asked if he thinks of himself as a *retired thief*, he immediately replies, "Well, what else? That's all I've done all my life." His statement is an exaggeration, as he did hold some legitimate jobs during his working life and operated his own business for a short time. But it is substantially correct. For the best part of 40 years, Jack worked as a burglar.

Jack was incarcerated first at age 14 for auto theft, an offense for which he claims innocence. He was committed to the state training school, an austere place where the treatment was harsh:

> Now, you see, at a tender age... you can build up a pretty good well of hate from being mishandled and abused.... And I'll guarantee you, when you came out of there, you would either never steal again or you didn't fear God himself.

Jack spent approximately 18 months in the training school. Several years after his release, in the depths of the Great Depression, he was sentenced to the state reformatory, again for auto theft. He was released after serving approximately two years.

Following his release from the state reformatory, Jack became serious about stealing. Until that time, his offenses were rare and generally an incidental result of youthful fun, playfulness, or trouble. As he tells it today, he was in the county jail for some reason and was passing time by playing poker with some other jail inmates, one of whom was a well-respected thief.

> [T]his guy, he was, locally, he was a pretty big man. Now, I don't mean he was a big man [in the sense] that he was a local Mafia figure, or an overlord, or something like that. But he was pretty well respected in the community, being a very capable man. He was a thief, ran gambling joints and after-hours joints and I was a young, stand-up kid. So, it was a kind of a *mutual* respect.

The two won all the money from their fellow inmates but then decided to return some of it so the others would be able to buy commissary items for the remainder of the week. This gesture impressed the older man. According to Jack, several weeks later the older man "pulls up in front of the house. Nice car. Went for a ride, went out and had dinner."

Jack began spending increasing amounts of time with the older man. Eventually, he was asked to serve as the driver on a burglary and this led to participation in further burglaries. However, he always remained outside while his confederates made the entry and did the inside work. (Jack says that in those days older thieves often were reluctant to teach younger men all their skills. They feared that the students eventually would have little need for their teachers.) However, on several occasions he was needed inside and was able to observe the others as they bypassed alarms and opened safes. Later still, Jack and his tutor planned to commit a burglary but the latter was unable to participate. He encouraged Jack to proceed as planned:

> So, I went in and attacked the damn thing [safe]. I got a local guy with me and bing, bing, bing and the damn door swung open. I liked to fainted: "Well, I'll be damned.... Look at that." ... I got a hell of a break, you know.... I *knew* what to do, but I didn't have any confidence in myself because I never tried it before.

Jack continued stealing with his older colleague, who had connections in several parts of the country. The two of them traveled and "worked" in many states. During a period of 25 years he was arrested often but managed to avoid incarceration on all but one occasion—he served three years for breaking and entering.

Jack was married and divorced during this period. He lived comfortably and spent his leisure time in the style of most thieves, traveling, gambling, and partying. Later he married again and secured legitimate employment. His marriage, job, and the birth of the couple's first child caused him to cease crime almost entirely:

> Right after my daughter was born I was working for a reputable company in town, making a living, getting along all right.... I could see myself looking forward to no problems.... And I was not what you would call *resigned* to my fate, I was quite content with it.

This interlude ended when Jack received a call from another thief who assured him that he knew where "there's *twelve tons* of money!"

> I said, "good, I'll be down." Well, you can't hold a responsible position and just take off when you want to, right? In *any* field. And I wasn't in a position where I was an executive or working in an office, where I got to have a couple of days off "to go visit my sick mother." It doesn't work that way. [So] I just weighed the job against the potential that I had to gain, and I had to quit.

By the late 1950s, Jack regularly received information about individuals who had made large sums of money illegally that they were hoarding (e.g., bootleggers, professional gamblers). He began to specialize in burglaries of this type and traveled throughout the United States in his work. At age 50 he and two other men traveled to one of the western states to commit a burglary. They checked into a motel and contacted their tipster. However, local police, alerted to the presence of suspicious persons at the motel, raided their room. The police found a combination of explosives and burglary tools. Despite their intentions, Jack and his colleagues had not yet committed a crime. Believing they were arrested and convicted wrongfully, they waged a lengthy legal battle to avoid incarceration. Eventually, an appellate court overturned his conviction, but the issue was moot by that point as he already had served four and one-half years in prison.

After his parole Jack secured legitimate employment and worked for nearly eight years until his retirement. He did not terminate his criminal activities entirely during the first few years after his parole, but he was involved in only a few burglaries. As time passed, these activities declined to the point that now he no longer participates. However, he still "thinks like a thief" and insists there remains the possibility that he will return to stealing. It would require an extremely large inducement, "but, still, I'll be honest enough to say that I could still be enticed, sure. Why, why should I fool myself?"

As Jack terminated direct involvement in burglary, the information he received from others, which is essential to the thief, changed in kind:

> I think when somebody contacts me now they want something. They don't want to *give* me something. Where, over the years before, they wanted to *give me* something. Of course, they wanted to acquire my expertise or ability or further connection into some other field. But now, it's *for* something; then, it was *to give* something.

Today the information he receives about potential burglaries has "diminished practically to a trickle."

Part of the reason for this is grounded in shared beliefs about age and the decline of one's capabilities. Thieves are no more immune from these assumptions and beliefs than are those in the straight world:

> [T]here's many things that a man 25 or 30 can do that a man 60, 65 can't do. He's much more flexible. He's quicker. . . . [T]he man of 30, he can outthink, outperform—he's got more strength, quicker witted, reflexes are 100% better than a man of sixty. . . . If you was going to have a major operation, now, would you go to a surgeon that is 65, or would you go to a surgeon that's 40? . . . [The younger surgeon] has learned later techniques. His hand is more sure, he is not stuck in a mold where he only does things one way. His mind is fresher . . . and still, he's not green because he's been practicing for, what, 10 years?

But if they no longer can play an active, direct part in scores as they age, some thieves and hustlers manage to shift roles in the social organization of crime. For example, the aging thief can search out potentially lucrative scores and pass along the information to others who can exploit it. Even as they taper their direct involvement in crime, "they always got their eyes open for some mark they can give somebody else that's still operating." As Jack says, even for aging thieves, "*somewhere*, along the line, they got—just to relay a phone message—*somewhere* they've got to get their finger in the pie." With time, however, even this type of involvement becomes less common as one's contemporaries die and old connections dry up.

An extremely self-reliant individual, Jack and his wife live today in a style that seems indistinguishable from that of most couples in which the husband labored as a blue-collar craftsman.

Johnny Price

I interviewed Johnny Price in the suburban home he shares with his second wife and stepdaughter. A distinguished looking man in his mid-60s, he was on parole at the time, having recently served nearly two years in prison. He drives a new luxury automobile and owns a farm in another state. His recent felony conviction was his first in more than 40 years, a remarkable record considering the fact that he has worked all that time as a card and craps hustler and con man.

Johnny was reared in the Southwest in a large, intact family. His father worked as a construction craftsman, but the family's size meant that family resources were very limited. Today Johnny speaks of both his parents as "good people," but dwells on the complete absence of open displays of affection in the home. During Johnny's late preteen years, oil was discovered on the family's land and their economic fortunes improved substantially.

Johnny did not progress beyond the fifth grade of school and spent his free time with a group of older boys, a "stealing clique," as he calls it now. At age 16, he was sentenced to the state reformatory after conviction for stealing chickens. During the Depression years, discipline was lax in many state prisons. Convicts gambled and hustled openly, and some earned large incomes from these activities. Possessing a reputation for integrity, Johnny was accepted by some convicts who were deeply involved in the prison's sub rosa economy. As he says, "I learned to hustle in the penitentiary."

> [When I was locked up the prison yard] looked like a casino . . . poker games and crap games everywhere you looked. So I just kind of fell into a clique there and got to running a game for the people, and one for myself. . . . On weekends there, well, hell, I'd make $100. . . . Hell, I never ate in the kitchen, I'd eat out of the canteen, steak and eggs . . . anything you wanted.
>
> Q: The people just gambled openly, huh?
>
> A: Oh yes, wide open, all over the yard.

In addition to gambling, the convicts organized a crafts industry:

> Everybody got into working leather there. See, we contracted leather work out—I never done any of it, but I was in with that—where we bought the leather, buy hide after hide. Make saddles, boots, purses, pocketbooks, any leather goods you'd want to make, we was making it. . . . We'd farm out the hide to make purses with. Next guy, over here, might be making pocketbooks. Then we'd make connection with the bootmen. And all that sold through the front office. All the tourists come through there, you know, and had a chance to buy it.

A few months after his initial release he was convicted of burglary and sentenced to the state penitentiary. Again, shortly after release he was sentenced to the same institution after conviction of grand larceny. This pattern was repeated one more time before Johnny, at age 22, was released from confinement a fourth time. He left his native state and moved to California. He worked for several weeks and hustled part time.

Johnny acquired both skills and contacts during his years in prison. A few weeks after moving to California, he met an acquaintance, a hustler, from his native state. He then began hustling full time, the occupation he practiced for the next 40 years. He did not hold another legitimate job until two years ago, when his parole officer pressed him to secure one as a condition of parole.

During his 40-year hustling career Johnny traveled widely over the United States, Canada, and other parts of the world. He states that he was highly successful at his trade and developed several innovations that eventually were adopted by other hustlers. During his hustling activities he acquired a personal reputation for honesty, integrity, and loyalty, which is a source of pride to him. Partly for this reason, at the peak of his hustling activities he received telephone calls daily from people in different sections of the United States wanting him to "come here and play, come here and do this, come here and play." He estimates that he earned several million dollars gambling, and today he owns property in several states and appears to be secure financially.

Unlike most thieves and hustlers, Johnny says that money means little to him, and he always has enjoyed the challenge of hustling successfully far more than the income it yields. Moreover, he has no hobbies. He does not drink alcohol. Hustling is also the only activity he finds challenging; it is the only activity from which he derives pleasure and satisfaction. He believes this explains why he, unlike most hustlers, never has "chilled up"; that is, lost his nerve and severely curtailed or quit hustling.

Together with another man, Johnny was arrested in the mid-1970s on a federal charge:

> Now [after my arrest] they gonna get the rundown on me, and get my record. [And they said], "Oh lord, this guy here has slid around, been doing this for 40 years. . . . Well, lookie here, he's

got a rap sheet this long, nothing but hustling and con and everything else." So, they said, "we gotta give him a little rest."

After two jury trials Johnny was convicted. He appealed his conviction, ultimately to the U.S. Supreme Court, and he paid nearly $100,000 in attorney's fees. In retrospect, he says that no amount of money could have won his freedom. Eventually, after approximately 18 months in federal prison, he was paroled and returned to live with his second wife.

Today, Johnny is extremely ambivalent about his lifestyle and personal circumstances. He loves and respects his wife, a strong woman, and she has had a decided influence on him—he even attends church with her. He has found love, emotional security, and acceptance from her and her children. At the same time, he feels almost as though he is incarcerated, and he misses the travel and hustling life. Although he has not retired from hustling, he definitely has reduced his activities, primarily because of being on parole.

A LOOK AHEAD

In succeeding chapters I examine stigma problems among aging ex-convicts; orientational and interpersonal changes that accompany aging; age-related changes in criminal decision making; and the interview subjects' contemporary reflections on their criminal careers, the prison experience, and beliefs about the nature of crime control in America. In presenting these materials, I distinguish between the experiences and interpretations of the three categories of offenders sketched in Chapter 1 and illustrated here.

3

ELAPSING TIME
AND PROBLEMS OF STIGMA

Doubtless, the identity of "ex-convict" is one that few Americans aspire to or regard as a badge of honor. More pointedly, it is an identity that most people probably view as disreputable or inferior. Such a "socially inferior attribute" (Page, 1984: 2) or *stigma* is believed important because it may be socially consequential for the individual who is so encumbered.

Supporters of labeling theory emphasize the importance of stigma as an element in the continuation of deviant activities and careers. They point to the critical part played by social control processes, both informal and official, in the development of stigma. Possession of a stigma is said to produce a variety of interactional problems for the person. In an exemplary capsule statement of the argument, Becker claimed that being in a deviant status such as an ex-convict becomes for the individual a "master status" that "exposes [him] to the likelihood that he will be regarded as deviant or undesirable in other respects" (1963: 33). In turn, the cumulative social and social psychological effects of stigma and stigma management were said to escalate the probability of additional, *secondary deviation*. Secondary deviation develops as deviants gradually organize their identity and self-concept on the basis of deviance (Lemert, 1951). In this chapter I describe and discuss some stigma experiences of ordinary property offenders and how they are transformed by the passage of time.

Goffman's definition of stigma (1963) retains its utility. He noted that on the basis of everyday interactional experience we develop assumptions about the kinds of people we likely will encounter in various situations. In time we come "to know," for example, that the employees we encounter at the supermarket will not be flatulent or pick their noses publicly. Given sufficient experience and time, we construct and maintain an array of these *virtual social identities* for the people we likely will meet in various situations. Consequently, when we encounter strangers in the situations of everyday life, we impute to them a social identity and interact with them on the basis of our assumptions about those "kinds of people." Stigmatized persons disrupt this cozy symmetrical process. They possess an attribute that represents a discrepancy between their virtual and their actual social identity. Possession of such an attribute makes the individual *discreditable* in face-to-face social situations.

All of the men I interviewed had lived with the personal identity of ex-convict for periods of time ranging from 20 to nearly 50 years. All were among the *marked* (Jones et al., 1984). Curiosity if nothing else caused me to explore how they have managed this fact. I asked them whether they feel ashamed of their criminal record. Of the 35 men who were asked this question, 15 responded "yes." I requested descriptions of the kinds of everyday situations in which they are most aware of being an ex-convict. Finally, I asked if having a criminal record has proven to be a handicap and how they manage knowledge about their ex-con status in face-to-face interaction.

DAILY ROUNDS AND SITUATIONAL ROLE IDENTITIES

The routine activities that make up our daily lives are distributed ecologically in diverse social settings. Many of us, for example, work, play, and sleep in different locations with different sets of interactional others. Each of us then may have a number of role identities that correspond to the diverse settings of everyday life such as the family, the workplace, and places of recreation and leisure. We present somewhat unique role identities in each setting. Consequently, each of us has a repertoire of identities that describe us.

The interactional salience of any particular role identity varies situationally (McCall and Simmons, 1966). In the workplace, for example, the role identity of spouse usually is not interactionally salient. It is important to bear this in mind in this discussion of the stigma problems of ex-convicts. Like most of us, they have a repertoire of role identities. The role identity of ex-convict is only a part of this larger repertoire.

Based on their reported experiences the subjects fall into two categories. On one hand, those who have put their crime years far behind them said that feelings of stigma and the felt necessity to manage it are not significant problems in their daily lives. They encounter few situations in daily life in which the identity of ex-convict is salient. This is because the identity of ex-convict decreases in personal and interactional salience as the number of years that separates the prison experience and the current life increases. Equally important, even in situations in which the ex-convict identity is salient, they rarely fear being discredited. On the other hand, those men who persisted in crime beyond their late 30s, compiling lengthy official records in the process, were more likely than the first group to report enduring, although modified, stigma problems. The bulk of the comments here are focused on the first group.

All stigmas are not alike. Goffman (1963: 4-5), for example, distinguished "abominations of the body," such as physical deformities; "blemishes of individual character," such as dishonesty; and categorical stigmas of "race, nation, and religion." Largely because they are not equally visible, the three types do not present the same management problems; some are more concealable than others (Goffman, 1963: 48; Jones et al., 1984: 27-36).

A major reason why stigma problems do not loom large in the subjects' experiences is because of the distinctive nature of their stigma. Because it is a *conduct stigma*, it is less visible, hence more concealable, than other types of stigma. It need not intrude during interaction. Unlike the physically deformed, for example, the ex-convict has substantial latitude to negotiate an acceptable situational identity. It was Goffman who pointed out that those with concealable stigma are *discreditable* whereas those with highly visible stigma are *discredited* (1963: 4).

The interview subjects suggested several additional reasons why they experience few enduring problems resulting from their earlier criminal involvement. The overwhelming majority of them came from underclass or from working-class backgrounds and several of them claimed that prison records are not uncommon for persons in those social strata.[1] Consequently, many people have some experience interacting with ex-convicts:

> I don't meet too many people who care one way or the other [about my prison record], really. Most of the people I know are familiar with jails. They're familiar with, they're from a society that knows all about jails. They've had cousins or brothers, or they've been in jail themselves. . . . Maybe they're completely honest, but they know the difference. And it doesn't make any difference to them if a person's been in jail.

Another man suggested that because of the sociotechnical nature of the blue-collar work world, a person's past is of less concern here than might be the case in other types of work. Because the fiduciary component of many blue-collar occupations is low, employers are not so acutely concerned about biography and character. One of my research subjects had worked as a skilled construction worker for more than 10 years. On such jobs, he said, the foreman doesn't care "if you come from Yale or jail," so long as one can do the work. He went on to say,

> I don't think bein' or having a criminal record affected [my ability to work], you know.... It's all in what you can do, you know, 'cause you don't have to fill out any applications, only a W-2 form. After fifteen minutes on the job the man knows whether he can make money with you or not. And all he has to worry about is how regular you're going to be, how dependable.... So I didn't have much difficulty.

Furthermore, some men said that it is not particularly unusual for blue-collar workers to encounter men with prison records on the job. Approximately 12 of the interview subjects had worked in construction at one time or another. One of them said,

> Sometimes [at work] you're sittin' around talkin' to dudes, and that's all the dudes be talkin' about.... Lot of dudes, you know, done some time... bricklayers and things. And they sit down at lunch time, you know, and they talkin' about [it].... So, you know, whole lot of people been in jail, you know.

By itself, this lack of novelty produces a lessened concern about their stigma on the part of ex-offenders.

Another reason for minimal concern with the social and interactional consequences of their criminal record is the number of years that have elapsed since their involvement in crime (i.e., mere passage of time). The salience of the ex-convict identity seemingly declines over time, along with concern that one may be discredited because of it:

> I don't think that anybody [in my neighborhood] knows about my past, to tell you the truth. I live over in Silver Spring, Maryland, and I don't think anybody knows. If they do they have never said anything. . . . The people I associate with and all, they know me as "nice-Ben, who-owns-a-restaurant," and they accept me. There has never been any . . . in my case it never has been a stigma or anything, as far as ever being ashamed of it, or I would be ashamed if people know. Because, see what I have done over the 20 years that I have been out, 21 years. I have reestablished myself in the community as a good citizen, as a good parent, and a decent businessman. So, it is no big thing.

In sum, both sustained, successful performance in nondeviant roles and the passage of time tend to erode the salience of the ex-convict identity as well as the degree to which it is experienced as discrediting.

At the same time, it is important to note that a substantial majority of the men claimed that in day-to-day interaction there seldom is the need or the opportunity to mention or discuss their criminal record. Asked if his neighbors know about his prison record, a 47-year-old subject responded,

> No, why should they know? I mean, I'm not just gonna walk up and say to somebody, "look, man, I've been in prison." How would that sound? [They'd say] "why he's a hell of a fella, ain't he? Come up here telling me all this stuff. I don't want to hear all that." That's what they'd say. Something happened 25, 30 years ago, something like that. That wouldn't sound right, would it?

I asked another subject if he has hidden the fact that he is an ex-convict. He responded by saying,

> Well, truthfully, the way I've been carrying myself, nobody ever had to ask me anything [about my prison record]. I've always—

even before then—been a "jokey-type" fella and I treat just about everybody nice. And so they really didn't have no reason to ask me.

Ex-offenders also express a belief that the years they subsequently have spent in legitimate and usually physically tiring work *entitles* them to expect the same courtesies and respect afforded those without their stigma. They believe that an established record of gainful employment far outweighs the potentially negative reactions occasioned by disclosure that one is an ex-convict. Some believe that it legitimately empowers them to expect that their past be interactionally out of bounds. Witness the remarks of a 72-year-old man who served five penitentiary sentences before "squaring up":

> Q: Does your prison record ever come up in conversations with people today?
>
> A: No. It's water beneath the bridge. They better not bring it up in front of me. I don't want to hear it.... 'Course, now it's been so long. There's a lot of [people] don't know, even. And the ones that do know it keep quiet. Nothing's said about it.

In response to the question whether he would worry about others' reaction if he disclosed his prison record, another man said,

> I wouldn't feel that it would be any of their business. I mean, you know, it [prison record] should have no bearing one way or another, something I did twenty years ago. Why should it have any effect on what I do right now, my performance today?[2]

Finally, I offer a more speculative note. Although no subject expressed it spontaneously, the general lack of concern about their stigma suggests to me also that an experience factor is at work. On the whole, the passing of time and interactional success in managing one's various identities seems to be accompanied by increased confidence in doing so. Persons with official records for ordinary property crimes not only learn how to manage their stigma but also gain confidence that they can do so successfully in most situations. This too seems to account for the general absence of stigma among these men. In time, therefore, the ex-convict identity recedes in salience and rarely intrudes in conversation:

> I'm not ashamed that I was in jail, but I don't volunteer, if the subject's not brought up. I ain't gonna say, "well, I've been in jail," or something like that. I'm not gonna walk into somebody's home and just say, "well, I've been in jail," without the subject being brought up. But if it's brought up, I won't try to hide it.

These remarks were echoed by another subject, who said that even among intimates there seldom is any need to mention or discuss one's criminal past:

> Q: Are your record and your prison experience ever discussed in your home?
> A: No, no.
> Q: You don't talk about it?
> A: No, well, for what reason? There's no reason to.

I do not mean in any way to deny the existence of the often severe problems faced by ex-convicts, especially in the first years after release from prison. Nonetheless, the foregoing observations suggest a general process of *stigma erosion* that accompanies successful performance in nondeviant roles. Over time this produces a sense of incremental *social margin* on the part of ex-convicts (Wiseman, 1970). It seems that the long-term process of stigma management bears some similarity to the way that many people eventually come to terms with their middle names. What seems during youth to be an embarrassment that crops up in conversation almost daily, by early adulthood becomes an aspect of the self that is somehow detached from one's principal situational identities. And whereas youth seem unable to avoid having their middle names become objects of general conversation and ridicule, by young adulthood many have learned a variety of interactional techniques for managing conversation about such embarrassing topics. The same is true of men with prison records. Several men related to me incidents in which they seemed to interact confidently, albeit precariously, on the edge between passing and disclosing their stigma. A 56-year-old subject told me that he is reasonably certain that his coworkers know about his prison record, although he prefers not to discuss it with others. Despite their efforts occasionally to make it a topic of conversation, he declines to take the bait:

> So the guys talk about a certain year, and I don't have nothing to say about that particular time, like '65, '63, 'bout what had went on in Washington. I don't have no, I can talk about any other area, but they notice I'm silent on that. [They] say, "oh man, you must have been in jail, you don't know what happened." Said, "you must have been in jail." So I say, "oh no, man, you got the wrong concept."

STIGMA MANAGEMENT

The foregoing comments generally confirm the obvious, that possession of a stigmatic attribute does not ensure interactional difficulties. Given the passage of years and successful performance in legitimate roles, the fact that they are ex-convicts creates few interactional problems for these men:

> Q: Is it difficult for you to keep your record secret?
>
> A: I don't care. Now, I don't mean to sound, you know, like my record don't mean nothing to me. . . . When I first came out, people ask me where I've been. I might tell them, "ah, I went to visit my sister in New York," or "my aunt in Florida." . . . I was

ashamed of it. But as I grew older, I found out that I'm not the only one that's been in jail. I can't hide that.... Once you accept the fact that going to jail ain't no mortal sin, unless you continue to do it morning, noon, and night, then you don't care what people know about your record.

So long as they deal with individuals on a face-to-face basis, men like this seem confident of their ability to manage stigma. Consequently, interactionally "messy" incidents are rare for ex-convicts who have put their criminality behind them.

But the number of occasions in everyday life when their ex-convict identity is salient without resulting interactional problems are more numerous. And in these situations ex-convicts intentionally may employ one or a variety of strategies to manage the information they give others about themselves. I discuss three possibilities: disclosure, conversation, and passing.

Disclosure/Conversational Contexts

Stigma is acknowledged openly in two ways. The marked may choose to disclose it for the first time to others who previously were not aware of it. Or they may elect to acknowledge or to discuss it openly with those who already are aware of it. In both instances the stigma is acknowledged only when the marked does not fear the interactional or other consequences of doing so.

Men employed in blue-collar jobs occasionally disclose voluntarily their criminal record:

> [There was] a dude workin' with me . . . [and] he was in the service [military]. And the service is almost like a penitentiary, you know, the food line and stuff like that, you know.... [At lunch one day][h]e say, "man, you know [this food line] be like in the Army. By the time I'd get up there the food would be cold,

you know." "Well," I said, "that's the same way it is in the penitentiary. Sometimes you get up there and you is the the last person [that] comes in.... The food is cold."... And he said, "you've been in the penitentiary?" And I said, "yeah, I've been in the penitentiary."

Although the ex-offender may be relaxed and unconcerned about disclosure, situations of this type may be marked by a degree of interactional awkwardness:

I got me a new trainee [on the job]. He was new about two years ago, a little, young white fellow.... He and I got to talking one day. He asked me about what I'd been, how long I'd been in [my line of work] and what I did before then. I just told him: "When I got out of jail and stopped stealing I had to knuckle down and work." But he didn't know, he didn't know whether he was— whether it was safe to ask why I went to jail or not. (Laughs) So I just told him: ... I look at the time that I spent in jail, I'm not proud of it by no means. But on the other hand, I'm not ashamed of it.

In one type of situation the ex-offender discloses because he feels an ethical obligation to do so.[3] Simultaneously, he may hope that disclosure will forestall future "surprises" or problems occasioned by an uncontrolled—usually a third-party—disclosure. For example, if the person plans a business venture with another, or plans to marry, he may disclose his past. The ex-convict hopes also that disclosure "up front" will show that his character fundamentally is decent and trustworthy. At least he hopes to win benefits for candor and honesty.

And what about the other situations, when a person's ex-convict identity becomes the basis for conversation with those who already know about it? The marked may choose to initiate the conversation, usually as a method of establishing his bona fides or as a way of building situational credibility. In the most commonly reported situation, the ex-offender does so in hopes of dissuading a friend or relative who shows signs of deepening entanglements with authorities or the law. Many of the men related experiences of this type:

> Q: Are there any situations in which you have volunteered to other people that you were in jail?
> A: Yeah.
> Q: Tell me about them.
> A: Well, they come up with either my son, who is 13 years old, or some close friend . . . when I see them heading in that direction that I headed in, where they could possibly end up with some jail time, where I would bring it up that *I* had been in jail. And that I knew what I was talking about.

There are risks in taking a public stand of this type, because the activist role may backfire. One man found that the recipient of his remarks chose to interpret them as a sign of hypocrisy:

> My cousin . . . she's got two boys who are teenagers now. So, they started playing a little game of stealing stuff out of stores, you know. So I wrote them a letter and I really put it down heavy about how it is in prison and what you got to go through when you first come in. You want to be a little girl, they'll make a little girl out of you, if you don't know somebody, you know. I really laid it down heavy to these boys. You know what the boys said to me: "Well, it can't be so bad, you keep going back." So what the hell was I going to say then?

An ex-offender has written of a similar response he received from his brother:

> The few times I did try to discourage him [from crime], he would say, "Man, when you was such and such an age, you did such and such a thing." What could I say? Because I had [Allen, 1977: 8].

Interactional problems such as this are much less likely to occur when the conversation is initiated by the other person, especially if he treats the criminal record and associated experiences as "background" or as "given." Apparently, many "squares" tend to see and to utilize the known ex-convict as an informational resource. Several men told me that they are viewed by family and friends as lay experts on the worlds of crime and imprisonment. A man who once used and sold drugs said,

> [G]uys at work, my coworkers, you know, have conversations sometimes. . . . [O]ne of them might come up to me and say, well, "man, my son had some stuff and it was brown, and in foil," and he said "I threw it away. But I should have brought it in so you could see. Tell me what it was, you know." And I say, "well, only could have been two things, you know." I say, "it could have been 'mud' or it could have been hash, you know." I say, "mud is a brown substance, dope in powder form." I say, "hash is a brown, cube-like lump of sugar, only smaller."

Often this occurs after friends or relatives have gotten into some kind of trouble with the law. Then they seek the ex-offender's counsel:

> Q: [Your nieces] all know you were in jail at one time?
>
> A: Right.
>
> Q: That doesn't make them avoid you, or anything?
>
> A: Uh uh. See, 'cause they'll come to me if something bothering them, they'd come to me and talk about it, you know, and shit like that. You know what I mean. They know I been there. . . . [One time] my niece had hooked school, you know, and they was in this house. . . . I don't know if they was housebreakin' or what. Anyway, they had no business in there, you know. She came to me, you know, and sat down and talked to me about it, you know.
>
> Q: Was she worried?
>
> A: Yeah, she wanted to know what should she do. . . . So I sat down and talked to her about it, you know.

Clearly, situations of this type pose no threat of discreditation.

Passing Contexts

Ex-offenders occasionally find themselves in situations in which they experience the ex-convict identity as salient and also fear that disclosure would be discrediting. Fearing the consequences of disclosure, either for themselves or for others, they stand ready to conceal their stigma. Thus, the probability of disclosure decreases as the perceived certainty of significant negative consequences increases. However, the felt necessity to pass rarely occurs. In fact, few of the men could recall occasions recently when they passed. One who did told me that he feared the potential consequences for his employment:

> I've got a good position. I'm under bond. I'm over a hundred thousand bond.... How would that bonding company feel if they found out that I was in prison? Man, they'd drop my ass in a minute.... I wouldn't dare talk about [my past] to anybody. I got a good position, I get good money. Hell, I'm living good, I'm eating good.

Since few of the interview subjects had passed recently, I asked them for examples of situations in daily life when their ex-convict identity simply became more salient to them, even though they didn't fear being discredited.

Spontaneous discussions of crime and imprisonment that often occur in the workplace were the most common answers. During data collection in Washington, D.C., a socially prominent physician was murdered when he unexpectedly encountered a burglar in his home. Subsequently it was learned that the offender had amassed substantial wealth in his nocturnal activities since escaping from a New York prison several years earlier. The incident received much media coverage. Several men said that the incident had prompted conversations at work about crime and imprisonment.

One of the problems posed by such spontaneous conversations is whether to respond to inaccurate or lurid assertions about offenders or the experience of imprisonment. Thus, a once imprisoned uncommitted offender said to me that during these discussions,

> [t]he hard part is to keep your mouth shut when people are on that subject [prisons].... [Say] something's in the paper and—especially Lewisburg [federal penitentiary]—a couple of times people talked about Lewisburg. And, you know, it's hard. I just thank God I'm successful in not saying a word, just listening. But it's hard. And a few times, too they were saying things that weren't really true, at least not as I knew them.

What is interesting in the subjects' accounts, however, is how infrequently they mentioned fear of being discredited as the principal reason they tend to avoid disclosure. Rather, they sometimes fear that the intended object of the advice might romanticize crime or the ex-offender. For this reason, one man has minimized conversations at his home about his prison experience. Not wanting to appear "unfatherly," or say anything that conceivably would appear to condone or to glamorize crime, he has preferred to say nothing about his crimes and imprisonment:

> Q: Now you said you have three children, right? Do they know you were in jail?
>
> A: Well, sometimes I think the little boys do, 'cause sometimes I get to talking about it and, well, [my wife] makes me shut up. I think she don't want them to really know too much about me bein' there. 'Cause the idea for some little boys is, they have a tendency to say, "well, I want to be just like dad.... Dad's been in jail so, bang, it's alright for me to go."

Others said they generally avoid disclosure because they would not want it to be seen as a form of bragging. They said they react with distaste when they hear others openly discussing their prison experiences:

> I don't think it's necessary to go around ... and say, you know, "I was, I done this, and I'm here, and look at me." I don't think

it's necessary. I watch some people on television some time—I know you've probably seen them on these shows. And they say, "well, I've done this and look at me now." I don't think much of it.

Having put behind them the persona to which the ex-convict identity applies, ex-offenders are not particularly threatened by disclosure. Nevertheless, a desire to avoid the hassles of being a known ex-convict is a major consideration in managing their stigma. Most of them simply wish to retain the autonomy and leeway to avoid uninvited, lengthy, and naively inspired questions.

As time passes, more often then not it is some "blemish of character" other than dishonesty that they fear would be signaled by disclosure. Having come to view their own youthful crimes as foolish and the years in prison as wasted, they fear being ridiculed by others for having been so foolish. Understandably, they do not want to become the involuntary objects of gossip and inappropriate comments from others. For all these reasons they prefer to restrict knowledge about their past and the interactional hassles that disclosure would entail:

> I don't want [my background] to become a topic of conversation. This is a private part of my life I don't want [my coworkers] to have.... It wouldn't do me no good, and it would do them, they would use it as a means of conversation, that's all, just gossip. They'd pass it on to every person they come in contact with, where I work. So, no, I would not want to talk to them about it for that reason.

PERSISTENT OFFENDERS

And what of those ordinary property offenders who persist in their criminality and usually spend many years in prison? Interestingly, the nature of their stigma changes over the years. Whereas they were stigmatized as "ex-convicts" when they were young, as they age they increasingly are stigmatized as "ex-convicts who have failed to desist from self-defeating behavior." As this process occurs, they run the risk of alienating the few remaining straight people with whom they maintain contact. A 50-year-old man who sleeps in a city shelter and shoplifts almost daily as his means of livelihood told me that even his mother and siblings finally have given up on him. The experiences of men such as these suggest a process of stigma transformation that develops when one fails to desist from crime.

Those offenders who persist at crime also discover eventually that other adverse biographical and personal factors assume increasing importance. In time, these may even supplant the stigma of being an ex-convict. This process makes it increasingly difficult for them to secure a stable, legitimate niche in the conventional social world. I asked one man if being an ex-convict has been difficult for him. He responded,

> About jobs, decent-type jobs. Especially when you get old, see. When I say "old," you know, I'm 54. So if I was 25 it wouldn't matter, see. When I first came out, it didn't make no difference 'cause they didn't care, 'cause I was qualified, and physically and mentally able, as far as the job was concerned. But now, when they look up and I take my hat off and they see the bald-headed old man here, they pass me.

For men such as this, advancing age, especially when it is coupled with declining physical condition and the absence of significant work experience, conspires to compound their original stigma.

THIRD-PARTY DISCLOSURE

When asked directly about the ways that having a criminal record has been a handicap in their lives, one type of answer was given more often than others. The men said it has handicapped them in dealing with bureaucracies that have, they believe, inflexible or other special policies for dealing with ex-convicts. At the very least, these policies may necessitate added time and hassles if the marked person is to gain a satisfactory outcome of his request or problem. One man, whose crimes occurred while he was in the Army, said that his dishonorable discharge made him ineligible for the benefits of the G.I. Bill. Another man discussed the problems he encountered when he tried to enlist in the U.S. Army:

> Q: Has that experience of having been locked up for three years had any negative consequences for you over the last twenty years?
>
> A: The only thing I can remember really having any trouble doing was getting in the service. And the reason I couldn't get in the service was because of my record, you know.

Eventually the Army accepted him, but only after he complied with special regulations. The interview subjects expressed irritation and regret, but little anger at such situations.

Several men told of incidents when disclosure by a third party, often a functionary in one of the social control bureaucracies, disrupted their comfortable patterns of stigma management. Men with official records of crime and imprisonment are aware that their correctional records probably are housed somewhere, in some file cabinet or government archive. Knowing or suspecting this, they also understand that circumstances beyond their control can produce a renewed confrontation with their past.

> Now, I haven't been in trouble since 1969. That was the last time I committed a crime. But if somebody would come break into my house, and I would shoot him, or something like that—and I would have to go to court for it—my past would be brought out, which isn't fair to me.

A 56-year-old man spoke of being stopped and detained by the police because of being in suspicious circumstances. After learning about his criminal record the detective informed his employer. The latter drove to the police station, only to discover that the subject's release was imminent:

> So they let me go. So we came on out and he dropped me off home, and told me he'd see me in the morning. He didn't say anything that day about it.... And [the next day] he told me, he said "what kind of police is that?" Said "he tell me about you had a record, did I know it, and why I let a man work with me with a record," and all that. So I played mum on him, to see what he was going to say. So that's when he said, "well, by you being an ex-convict, so what?" Said, "I'm going to treat you right. How you going to treat me?" I said, "I'm going to treat you right." And after that it was never mentioned again.

Another man, employed as a chauffeur, related a similar incident. He had been given a set of keys to one of his female customers' homes. While police were investigating an attempted burglary of the home they discovered his criminal record and informed her of the fact. His account of the subsequent interactional dynamics shows how awkward it can be to deal with stigma when an additional component of felt betrayal is involved:

> So then when she confronted me with it, she said, "Uh, I didn't know you had a police record." I said, "you never asked me." She said, "well, that's true." She said, "well, do you have one?" I said, "yes, I do." She said, "do you want to tell me about it?" I said, "do you want to know about it?" So she said, "no, I don't." So, later—one, maybe two or three weeks later—I asked her, "would you like to know about it, or do you want your keys back, or anything?" She said, "no." She said, "because if you was going to take anything, you'd have taken it by now."

These incidents of third-party disclosure are more troublesome than the interpersonal problems created by their own voluntary disclosure of their criminal records. *Spreading stigma* (Studt, 1973) in ways such as these causes anger and bitterness, especially when it apparently is done with intent to harm the ex-offender. A self-employed businessman told me of problems he encountered when he sued a person over a failed business venture:

> So we went for a deposition with his lawyers and mine, see, and they brought up, "Well, have you ever been in prison? Weren't you put in prison for bank robbery?" . . . They knew, they knew. How they found out, I don't know, you know. It just shocked me when they asked me. Well, rather than go through court and have all that come out, and hurt me, I just had to drop it. . . . I was in business, I couldn't afford . . . [to] have all that come out in court.

Ex-offenders understand, although they resent, the special policies of bureaucracies that seem to relegate them to second-class citizenship. But they particularly resent and are angered by the personalized nature of some of the incidents that occur. A 42-year-old man told of receiving a routine prescreening questionnaire for jury duty. He completed the questionnaire—it asked specifically if he was a convicted felon—and returned it to the court clerk. A mixup ensued. After receiving several increasingly threatening letters, he went to the clerk's office to straighten up the problem:

> [I said to the clerk] "Why do you keep sending me these threatening letters, about marshals coming and picking me up and locking me up for not answering your inquiries?" "Well, sir you have no rights." . . . He comes out of his mouth, says "a convicted felon like you has no rights, sir, you have to fill that out again." I said, "I have one right. I have the right to grab you in the collar and snatch you across that damn counter. Now you call me something else, hear!"

Fortunately, even a bureaucracy's ability to keep track of stigmatized individuals is imperfect. Recall that Lonnie Eaton never has disclosed his criminal record for fear that it would jeopardize his employment. He also has been through two security checks, and in neither case was he challenged. Two other men related similar experiences.

STIGMA DISAPPEARANCE?

None of the observations to this point is meant in any way to minimize the nature and severity of the problems faced by ex-convicts in the short run. As for stigma problems over a longer period of time, they appear to diminish substantially as the ex-offender distances himself from that identity. Parenthetically, I believe this in part explains why the subjects were curious, but rarely fearful, when I contacted them initially about the research project.

As I returned to labeling theory for clues to some of the stigma problems potentially faced by my research subjects, I was struck by the severely truncated temporal dimension of stigma and stigma management sketched in the labeling theoretical literature. We typically encounter the stigmatized already bearing his or her full burden, with no significant past history other than contact with agents of social control. In a vague and never fully elaborated sense, the future was projected as a continuation of this pattern, perhaps in the form of an ever-deepening spiral of difficulties. Labeling theory paid little attention to the possibility of temporal improvement in managing stigma problems. Labeling theorists placed so much emphasis on the burdens borne by the stigmatized individual that they failed to acknowledge the possibility of *temporal* variation. Instead, the only variation permitted was *situational.*

But if the experiences of these ordinary property offenders are any indication, it may be useful for us to pay increasing attention to long-term transformation of the process of stigma management. Some have suggested that *disappearance* may be the final stage in the process of managing some kinds of stigma (Jones et al., 1984). Given the paucity of research on the process, this assumption may be both hasty and unwarranted. For the present, however, it does seem that stigma changes by a process of erosion, at least for those ordinary property offenders who have put their crime years behind them.

NOTES

1. I failed to question the subjects specifically about cross-class interactional experiences, and the interview data contain no mention of special problems in such situations.

2. Not surprisingly, and as the remainder of this chapter shows, this expectation is not honored in all situations. It is possible, therefore, to think of the prison experience as analogous to borrowing money at usury. Often the principal (imprisonment) can be amortized quickly enough, but the interest (stigma problems) may require a lifetime to repay.

3. Legislators and other officials have provided special penalties for failure to disclose one's ex-convict status in some situations (e.g., when applying for certain kinds of employment or when applying for a passport).

4

ORIENTATIONAL AND INTERPERSONAL CHANGES

Although we have known about the inverse aging-crime relationship for more than a century now, we have few explanations for it. Sheldon and Eleanor Glueck (1937) explained this relationship by a hypothetical process of *maturation*.[1] Our explanatory efforts have not progressed appreciably beyond their work. As Wooton notes, this is "one of the—unhappily not infrequent—occasions on which a label has been mistaken for an explanation" (1959: 164).

If we are to develop an understanding of the link between aging and decreasing criminal involvement, follow-up studies of offenders at various stages of the life course may prove especially revealing. There are three types of previous longitudinal research on adult offenders.[2] Traditional parole prediction research exemplifies one of these. Official records are analyzed statistically to determine which variables differentiate parole "successes" and "failures." Usually a short follow-up period of three or four years is employed, although occasionally a longer period is used (Mattick, 1960; Kitchener et al., 1977). Generally, these studies are atheoretical, being stimulated by technocratic, correctional concerns and assumptions. Their findings are of limited value for efforts to interpret the aging-crime relationship.

A second genre of follow-up studies combines the use of official data with interviews of offenders or former offenders in order to identify variables that differentiate them with particular criminal career characteristics. Much of this research is dictated by correctional concerns, but some of it has been conducted to develop more general knowledge of criminal careers (e.g., Petersilia et al., 1978). Other investigations are guided by theory-generating or theory-testing objectives (e.g., Glaser, 1964; Erickson et al., 1973; Waller, 1974). Although many have used personal interviews with offenders or exoffenders, these tend to be highly structured in order to elicit comparable data from all subjects. Most studies of this type have used a short follow-up period, although there are some notable exceptions (e.g., Glueck and Glueck, 1937; Reitzes, 1955; McCord and McCord, 1969; McCord and Sanchez, 1983).

Investigations of a third type are guided primarily by theoretical interest, and usually employ a relatively unstructured, inductive interview methodology to understand and depict the fates and careers of offenders from their vantage point (e.g., Ray, 1964; Finestone, 1967; Irwin, 1970; Bull, 1972; Waldorf and Biernacki, 1979, 1981; Waldorf, 1983; Ward and Schmidt, 1983; Cusson, 1984). Some of these studies have used a rather short follow-up period, and several were done on incarcerated subjects (e.g., Stebbins, 1971; Frazier, 1976; Meisenhelder, 1975, 1977). Nevertheless, a distinguishing characteristic of this research is a willingness to treat the offender or ex-offender as an intelligent, self-aware informant rather than a passive subject. The principal objective in research of this type is development of an interpretive understanding of experiences that produce alternative career outcomes.

The methods and objectives of the present research are similar. I focused on identifying changes experienced by aging offenders that seemingly explain modifications of their criminal behavior. These changes are described here and in Chapter 5.

Offenders describe two broad categories of experiential changes that accompany aging: *orientational* and *interpersonal*. Although most of the men in the sample were 35-40 years old when these changes occurred, there was substantial variation in the matter. For some men they occurred in their late 20s; however, one member of the sample was in his 60s when they occurred.[3]

When asked if they "had changed over the years," virtually every man responded affirmatively. Some did so in emphatic, unequivocal terms:

> Practically all my life I was in some kind of an institution.... And they called me *"incorrigible."* I laugh at it now: "incorrigible." I couldn't be changed.
>
> Q: Why do you laugh at it now?
>
> A: Because they're *"experts,"* they're experts. And they're supposed to be able to analyze a person and come up with the exact answer. There was nothing that could be done with me. I would never change. I *have* changed.

Aging ordinary property offenders describe, albeit in a variety of terms, experientially subtle but fundamental changes they can see in themselves. They said they had become "more settled," "more mature," "softer," or "more responsible."

> You mellow down, you see. You put more emphasis on stabilizing yourself, you know, planting yourself in one place and not thinking that you are the center of attraction.

Others spoke of becoming more "reasonable":

> My trouble came from defiance—see—of authority.
>
> Q: Do you still have that in you today?

A: No, I don't have that in me. I like to think of myself as being a reasonable person, and being able to cope with situations. [I try to] use some logic and common sense, see. If there's something I don't understand, I'll try to get to the bottom of it. This is my trend of thinking now.

Men employ these linguistic labels to designate fundamental subjective changes that they perceive in their self-concept, their motivations, and their characteristic approaches to problem solving. Because they shape one's elemental approach to a wide range of everyday situations and to others, changes of this type are *orientational* in nature.

On the other hand, the interviews revealed a number of more specific changes that men frequently cite as indicators of these overarching orientational changes. The interview subjects pointed to these changes as more comprehensible, explicable indicators of the larger ones. Consequently, these specific contingencies represent the experiential core of orientational change.

SPECIFIC ORIENTATIONAL CONTINGENCIES

During their late 30s to early 40s, men who have not desisted from ordinary property crime begin to take stock of their lives and their accomplishments. In the process, they squarely confront the realization that (1) their criminality has been an unproductive enterprise, and (2) this situation is unlikely to change. In short, they realize that ordinary property crime is a dead end:

I was thinking about it not too long ago. And it seems like you reach a certain age, and you look back, and it seems like all your life you were chasing that pot of gold—at the end of the rainbow. And you reach a certain age, and when you look back, there ain't no pot of gold, really. And the *rainbow* is gone. And then where to from here?

As part of this stock-taking process, they experience one or more of four orientational contingencies: (1) a new perspective on the self; (2) a growing awareness of time; (3) changes in aspirations and goals; and (4) a growing sense of tiredness. Of the 30 unsuccessful offenders not in prison, 27 reported one or more of these changes.

A New Perspective on the Self

As they get older, ordinary property offenders develop and employ a critical, detached perspective toward their earlier years, behavior, and the personal identity that they believed it exemplifies. They gain a vantage point—in Archimedes' terms, "a place to stand"—from which they can view and critique their behavior and self. What they describe is nothing less than development of a separate, evaluative, judgmental perspective. A 56-year-old man described this experience:

> I saw myself for what I really was. I saw what I was. I saw it. With my own eyes I saw myself. I could see it just as plain as I'm looking at you now. And I know that what I looked at was a sorry picture of a human being. . . . I was a self-made bastard, really.

A former English thief describes a similar experience:

> I realized that the thoughts that were going through my mind were the thoughts of another person, and I began to look inwards at myself. I began to see the change that was taking place in me. . . . It was as if I was looking at someone I had known, someone who had been a habitual criminal [Wilson, 1964: 118].

Parenthetically, acquisition of an altered perspective on their youthful self and activities sometimes makes it difficult for ex-offenders to answer questions without first qualifying their answers. I asked several men if there was anything they could recall that they liked about doing time. One man responded by saying,

> Maybe I did. There's some things I might've liked, because I got a lot of recognition. I was, you know, accepted. Maybe I liked that part about it . . . but, see, I'm tryin' to put two things together. In my thinking *now* I can't see *nothing* that I can say I enjoyed. But, probably then I did.

Another man echoed these comments:

> In retrospect I would say I wasted [my earlier years]. But during that time I thought that, for me, it was productive. But now I can look back and say it's wasted, 'cause all I gained from those years is experience and knowledge on how not to act no more, you know, how to keep out of trouble. But during that particular time, anything somebody say, "boom, I'm ready to go," you know.

Development of an evaluative perspective on the self is not unique to aging offenders. Many aging nonoffenders also develop a detached, sometimes wistful, perspective toward their youth.

Employing their new perspective, aging offenders gradually view their youthful self as "foolish" or "dumb":

> Hey man, everybody got the nature to want to live good, you know, a desire to live good. And I thought that was the best way to do it, you know, by stealing, you know. I could get things that I ordinarily couldn't get by working. But, man, now I don't look at it that way. I think I was stupid.

This new perspective symbolizes a watershed in their lives. They decide that their earlier identity and behavior are of limited value for constructing the future.

Some men are bedeviled by an inability to account for this change, but others point to several experiences that they believe facilitated its eventual arrival:

> I was making comparisons between myself and those who was around me. You see, it's like looking in a looking glass when you see someone else like you. And I had a whole lot of them around that was like me.

Others spoke, sometimes poignantly, of the availability of dead time in the prison as a vehicle they utilized to construct this new perspective (Meisenhelder, 1977). A 46-year-old former addict said,

> I had a lot of time to think. Every time you go to jail—all right, all day long I'm running around playing with dudes—but think about them nights. Man, I'd be in them cells. I got to be by myself and can't go to sleep. I got to think, and if you sit down and think enough, something's going to come to you . . . first thing, you going to start trying to figure out things.

The aging process of ordinary property offenders, then, includes a redefinition of their youthful criminal identity as self-defeating, foolish, or "stupid."

Growing Awareness of Time

While taking stock of their lives, men become acutely aware of time as a diminishing, exhaustible resource. As one man said, "I did not observe the value of *time* until I was damn near

46 or 47 years old." After achieving this new perspective he, like others in the sample, began constructing plans for how to use the remainder of his life. The future now becomes increasingly valuable, and the possibility of spending additional time in prison especially threatening. A 45-year-old parolee said he did not want to serve any more time in prison. Asked if he was "afraid of doing time now," he replied,

> No, I'm not really afraid of it. I don't know, I just don't want to do it. . . . It's just knocking time out of my life.
> Q: Are you trying to say that the years you have left are more precious to you?
> A: True. And they're a lot more precious to me than when I was 25 or 30. . . . I guess you get to the point where you think, well . . . you're getting old, you're getting ready to die and you've never really lived, or something. You don't want to spend it in the joint, treading water.

Similar comments were made by a man who was interviewed in prison:

> I'm older [now] and I don't have much time. I guess you start looking at how much time you have left, and what to do with that time. . . . I'm 42 now. I got 20 years left and I'm setting here doing this dead time. You know, nothing out of my life but dead time. . . . Every year that goes by, it seems like it's quicker, you know. Life, before you're 21 it seems like it's forever, before you turn 21. And after you do, time seems like it's flying by.

Increasingly aware now that the remaining years of their lives are passing, aging men dread receiving a long prison sentence. Yet they fear that because of their previous convictions, any prison term they might receive will be lengthy. Not only would another prison sentence subject them to the usual deprivations, but it would expropriate their few remaining, potentially productive years. They fear losing their last remaining opportunity to accomplish something and to prepare financially for old age. Like many subjects, one man said he did not want to spend any more time in prison because "when I come out of there, that's *it*."

> Q: What do you mean, "that's it?"
>
> A: I'd be old, you know.... The whole world be done passed me by, man.

The same man went on to say,

> Hey, I'm 47, you know. And if I get one of them big numbers [long sentences] now, hey, I'm through bookin', you know. I'm through bookin'.... One of them big numbers, man, would do me in, you know. And I could not stand it.

The growing awareness of time as a limited resource intensifies fears of dying inside prison:

> Man, the time, I didn't pay no attention to time [when I was younger]. They give me time, man, I just went in there and did the time and come on right out. And man, didn't give it no thought. I'd go right back and [commit crime].... [Now] I'm gettin' older. Hey man, I ain't *got* to make it. See what I'm sayin'?
>
> Q: No, I don't know what you mean. You "haven't got to make it."
>
> A: I'm gettin' *older*.... As a young man I had a better chance of livin' and gettin' out.... I've seen dudes die in the penitentiary.... I don't know what it is, something make me think about things like that now.

Changes reported thus far by aging ordinary property offenders bear some similarities to age-related changes reported by nonoffenders. Neugarten (1968) discovered that males consistently change their time orientation as they age, restructuring life in terms of time-left-to-live rather than time-since-birth. Her subjects also developed a new perspective on the self as they got older. Findings from Levinson's study of middle-aged males (1978) also appear to be consistent with the experiences of aging offenders. As they got older, Levinson's subjects became increasingly introspective. They began unmasking illusions about themselves and evaluating their lives in terms of relative success or failure. Increasingly, they became future oriented and thought about the inevitability and approach of death.

There may be some differences in the findings as well. For example, Levinson's hypothetical stages or "seasons" of life may not apply easily to the lives of aging criminal offenders. Both Neugarten and Levinson used interview samples disproportionately composed of middle-class, professional men. The latter acknowledges that this tilts his "sample as a whole toward the higher end of the class structure in terms of social origins" (1978: 12). Neugarten's findings show that the changes reported by her subjects occur earlier in the life course for men from working-class backgrounds—the background of most offenders. Perhaps this explains why her subjects, unlike the men interviewed for this research, were in their 50s when the reported changes occurred. Despite these interpretive cautionary notes, however, the experiences of aging offenders and nonoffenders appear strikingly similar in several ways.

Changing Aspirations and Goals

Aging ordinary property offenders also modify some of their aspirations and goals. Eventually they no longer feel they want or need to strive for the same level of material fulfillment and recognition they sought when younger. An ex-offender has written,

> I've got to a point where things that were important to me twelve, fifteen years ago aren't important now. I used to have a lot of ambitions, like everybody else has—different business ventures, stuff like that. But today, why, with what I have to

buck up against, why, I could be just as happy and just as satisfied with a job that I'm getting by on, where I knew I wasn't going to run into trouble or anything [Martin, 1952: 277-278].

And a 46-year-old interview subject said:

Hey man ... I like fine things, you know. I'd like to have me a nice automobile and—see, I don't have no automobile, man, you know. At one time I used to dress, man I used to love fine clothes and things, you know. I don't have that shit no more. ... It's not going to worry me ... because me throwin' bricks at the penitentiary to obtain this? I'll never have it.[4]

Just as important, aging men revise their aspirations. They begin assigning higher priority to goals that formerly were less important:

The things I like to do, they don't require having a million dollars. I like to do things, I like to walk. Many times, down by the Tidal Basin, Jefferson Memorial, I see people walking. I see people out there fishing. These are things I like to do. ... Just like the song says, "the best things in life are free."

Like the middle-aged nonoffender, an interest in such things as "contentment," "peace" and harmonious interpersonal relationships becomes more important to them:

I've thought about having a lot of things tangible. But I know these things will not really make me happy. ... I've been over in Crystal City ... a coupla' days in the past week. You look at those structures [buildings], and they are very beautiful, you know. But ... what is it if people are not at peace with themselves?

Referring to his earlier activities, a 56-year-old man said,

I don't want to live that kind of life no more. I want peace. I want joy and harmony. I want to be with my children and my grandchildren. I got a bunch of grandkids, and I want to be with them. I want to be with my mother. And when she passes on—I was in prison when my daddy died, I got to come home for five hours in handcuffs to see him—and when my mother passes on, I want to be there with her.

This man's newly kindled interest in family members is not unique. Other men revealed similar sentiments which, they acknowledged, developed only as they approached or attained middle age. Indeed, it is but one indicator of a larger change: a growing interest in and desire for intimate social relationships.

Simultaneously, the world of legitimate employment assumes a new attractiveness. Aging men realize that they can achieve their revised aspirations on a modest income, so long as it is consistent and predictable. Several men spoke of achieving the realization that they actually could support themselves in the free world by legitimate work. One man said that in his early years of imprisonment,

> I was defiant to the point of not having no one to change me.... But I changed those thoughts when I was in Alcatraz. And I realized, after I became a tailor, after I was in the upholstering shop, that if I got in the street, I said, I could make a nice living.

Released from prison in their 30s or early 40s, men such as this experience a heightened sense of urgency about securing gainful employment:

> It's a little late in life to accomplish something now. About the only thing I can hope for now is that I'll be able to get a little Social Security built up. And try to get something saved up for old age.
>
> Q: Do you feel like life's passed you by?
>
> A: No, I don't feel like it's passed. But I'm feeling like it's catching up with me awful quick and I haven't got anything to show for it.

Consider the remarks of an imprisoned thief:

> I've had some good jobs in my life, but I could never get one again. I'm getting too old now. When I was a kid, I had some

real good jobs. But if I could get a good job with a future to it, I'd probably square up. But now when I get out, I'm going to be forty years old—I'm thirty-seven now—and when I get out, I can't wander around from filling station to filling station. I've got to get out and make me some money [Jackson, 1969: 235].

Those who manage to find secure legitimate work begin to appreciate the advantages of a job with benefits such as sick leave and a pension. A 56-year-old man said,

> I'm satisfied now, you know. There ain't nobody can get me to do nothin' [commit a crime]. Not now. Not the way I'm goin' now. . . . Every year I go away on vacation. I got three weeks now. Next year I get four weeks. Yeah. So I'm happy, you know, right now.

Even those who continue their criminal activities often are content with committing less hazardous offenses, even if this means accepting smaller economic rewards.

Growing Sense of Tiredness

Sustained involvement in criminal activity demands much of the offender. Obviously, one must live with the fear of arrest and long-term confinement, and there are a variety of other problems as well. The commission of some crimes exposes one to the risk of serious personal injury or death. One must deal routinely with other people who may prove unreliable or treacherous for one reason or another. The person who is known as a successful thief or hustler may appear as a desirable target of the criminal designs of others. This necessitates constant vigilance. Crime partners may talk too much and to the wrong people:

> You never know when something might backfire on you, and you're going to get arrested. As careful as you could be, something could occur. . . . And while I was worried, I was

worried about what *somebody else* was going to say, 'cause that's how 90 percent of your information is telescoped to the police department.

If arrested, crime partners may bargain with the prosecutor, giving up others in return for more lenient treatment. Over a long period of time, contending with all these problems takes its toll on the offender:

> [Y]ou get tired. You get tired trying to be a tough guy all the time. People always expecting this and that [Allen, 1977: 106-107].

Asked why he had abandoned crime, one man answered succinctly:

> Being tired, you know. Just collapsing, that's all. I'd say age made me weak, made me tired, you know. That's all.

Like him, other offenders eventually grow tired of the problems of criminal involvement and the repercussions once arrested.

Beyond these blanket statements, it is difficult—in most cases impossible—for aging offenders to provide a more explicit, readily comprehensible statement:

> I really don't know why I went straight. I just decided that after I got out. It wasn't fear of the law, it isn't fear of the penitentiary, 'cause I've sat down and thought it out very seriously, but I just had enough of it, that's all [King, 1972: 158].

It is clear, however, that aging offenders begin to experience the criminal justice process, especially imprisonment, as an imposing, irksome accumulation of aggravations and deprivations. They grow tired of the problems and consequences of criminal involvement.

Some offenders develop a detached analytic view of the entire criminal justice system (Braly, 1976). They come to see it as an apparatus that clumsily but relentlessly engorges offenders and wears them down:

> [A]t 8 a.m. [on the day of my release], one of my keepers yelled, "McGregor, get your shit and get out, we need your cell."
>
> "What the hell do you need my cell for?" I cracked. "It's just like the other twenty-two hundred here."
>
> The "answer" was standing right outside my bars, wearing oversized coarse prison grays and a scared-to-death expression. I said hello to the new nigger waiting to take my place. . . .
>
> I could see the young brother's eyes jump with the same kind of hatred that used to keep my ass in the box, so I spoke to him, man-to-man. . . . "I ain't even gone yet, and already they got you to take my place. . . . It's taken me twenty-seven years of jailin' to learn that I am needed to do more than fill a shitbowl in some damn institution" [Sopher, 1978: 368].

A 57-year-old man said that he never committed and would never again attempt the "big score," the one highly lucrative crime that would permit him to retire in comfort. Asked why he had given up this dream of many thieves, he said, "Because I know how the system is. . . . The system is bigger than me." Similarly, another man said, "I got tired of doing time for little small things, and serving such a long priod of time. I got tired."

Occurrence of orientational change, as evidenced by one or more of the four contingencies, is consequential for ordinary property offenders in two ways. First, it produces a sense of disenchantment with the activities and lifestyles of their youth. This is evident, for example, in the succinct comments of one man discussing his second release from prison:

> I had already been convinced that I couldn't beat the system anyway, you know. What I was doin' wasn't gettin' nowhere, you know. It was just a dream.

They also become increasingly ready and willing to "give something else a try."[5] Now there is an interest in and a readiness for fundamental change in their lives:

> All I want to do is just be happy and, you know, be content. Try to stay in the street, you know, try to get me a job. 'Cause I know—[age] 51—I ain't got too much longer to be here. I hope I'll be here until my hair gets white as this paper. But I know, at 51, I can't be runnin' in an' out of those penitentiaries.

At this point the offender experiences, simultaneously, a sense of liberation and apprehension. The former because it signals a break with the past, the latter because many subjects remain uncertain whether they can construct a satisfying life free of criminal involvement.

Occurrence of interpersonal change provides a more extended set of change incentives. Interpersonal contingencies are establishment of a personally meaningful tie to (1) one or more conventional others (such as a woman) or (2) lines of activity.

INTERPERSONAL CONTINGENCIES

When they are young most men have close involvements with girlfriends, lovers, or spouses. By the same token, most try their hand at legitimate employment for varying periods of time. In both these respects they are little different from older men. What does distinguish young and older men in these areas is the meaning and personal significance of intimacy and employment.

Several men acknowledged retrospectively that they held potentially rewarding and satisfying jobs earlier in their lives but they did not appreciate this at the time. As a youth, one man secured work at the U.S. Government Printing Office, where an older employee wanted to teach him how to mix and to use inks:

> I said to myself [that] I didn't even want to be there. As much as possible, I went into the men's restroom and went to sleep. And I was glad to get out of there when it was time to get off. And I wound up resigning the job.

With the benefit of hindsight, he said that it was an excellent opportunity, one that he squandered.

Despite their involvements with women when they were younger, the interview subjects said that these were not important influences on their behavior. Instead, these were often exploitive relationships of convenience:

> I remember one time, man, if a broad couldn't get no money—I'm gonna show you how stupid people used to think. If a girl couldn't get no money, you know, or wasn't sellin' no pussy, bringin' me some money, hey man, she couldn't have me. Isn't that a hell of a thing for a mother fucker to say, "she couldn't have me?"

Some men spoke about the changing meaning of family ties as they aged:

> I have a daughter-in-law [and] a pretty fair son. He's never been arrested. I think I owe, I have a debt, you know, owe these people a debt, you know.... I feel that I should be dedicated to try to erase some of this bullshit that's been, ... what you call it? Negative thinking.

Aging, then, produces an intensified interest in employment and also in supportive and satisfying social relationships. Actually building such a relationship represents an interpersonal contingency in the offender's life.

Ties to Another Person

The establishment of a mutually satisfying relationship with a woman is a common interpersonal contingency. Of the 30 unsuccessful subjects not in prison, 7 mentioned this, either alone or together with other contingencies, as an important factor in the transformation of their career line:

> When I reached the age of 35 it just seemed like my life wanted to change. I needed a change in life, and I was tired of going to jail. And I wanted to change my life and stay out here. And by meeting the woman that I met it just turned my life completely around.... When I met her it just seemed like something in my life had been fulfilled.

Another man, who still engages occasionally in property crimes, said he once had stopped committing crimes entirely while living with a woman:

> I started living with this woman, you know, and my life suddenly changed.... I was contented, you know, bein' with her.... I cared about her, you know. I wanted to be with her, you know. That was it.... And, hey, I just found enjoyment there.

A 56-year-old man, separated from his wife at the time of the interview, talked about her influence on him during earlier periods of unemployment:

> I loved my wife—I love her still—and she talked to me a lot.... And if it wouldn't been for her, no tellin' where I'd be at, 'cause I'd most likely had a gun in my hand and robbed a bank or something. Or took something from somebody to get some food, you know.... She helped me along.

The social relationship resulting from this interpersonal contingency assumes a special importance. It provides the older man a secure social niche.

Ties to a Line of Activity

Immersion and successful involvement in a legitimate activity functions much like establishment of a relationship with another person. Several different types of activities were mentioned.

Two men said that religious experiences and the attendant close social relationships functioned in much the same fashion (e.g., Pollock, 1976).

Five of the 30 unsuccessful offenders indicated that having a satisfying job, either alone or combined with other experiences, was an important influence in their lives. As their perspectives change with age, legitimate employment, like personal intimacy with others, assumes more importance. For example, a 56-year-old man remembered when, as a younger man, he was interviewed for a job with a beauty and barber supply company:

> The guy liked me from the jump. And that's when I hooked up with him. And I went straight a long time *without the intentions* of going straight.... That was one turning point in the later part of my life.

A 48-year-old man recalled his experiences 17 years earlier:

> When I got out [the second time]... I sold a suit for $10 and I bought [some tools], just the bare necessities of what I needed, and I met a guy who carried me on the job.... So at that time I could make $160 a week.... And so, with this earning power I didn't have—I didn't have to steal... So this was right down my alley.

Another man told how enrollment in a college program affected him:

> I was learning things I didn't know anything about. And I'm not saying I liked all of it, you know, but I worked at it. And I think for the first three quarters I had a 4.0, and that made me

feel good, the whole self-concept, you know, kind of thing. . . . Plus, some of the classes I really enjoyed. . . . And so I kind of got into it. I liked it.

But regardless of how they acquire it, the interpersonal contingency is extremely consequential for the ex-offender. Successful participation in a personal relationship, a job, or some other conventional line of activity provides personal rewards and reinforces a noncriminal identity. A 47-year-old man told of changes that occurred after he met a woman:

> Through her I met a whole lot of straight people, you know, that I enjoyed bein' around, you know. Like her people, her parents, her sisters and brother, you know, her mother. I enjoyed bein' around them. And they was straight, you know, never been incarcerated, never been affiliated with the law, and shit like that. I enjoyed bein' around them, because they did some things—like, we played cards, played little games, you know. I like sports, you know; we'd sit down and talk about sports, and do things of that nature.

Development of commitment (Becker, 1962) in someone or some line of activity generates a pattern of routine activities—a daily agenda—which conflicts with, and leaves little time for, the daily activities associated with crime. I asked a 48-year-old man if his former crime partners ridiculed him after he "squared up."

> No. See, I spent very little time with these people anyway. By me working during the week, I might see them on the weekend. . . . Everybody knew that I was a bricklayer, that I was making good money, that I didn't have to [commit crimes].

And a 46-year-old former addict told me,

> [At] one time, man, I used to come down the street, right? All right, dudes run to me and hold conversation, you know: "Hey, John," so and so. They gonna talk about something. . . . At one

time we could always, they'd see me and they'd talk about what, you know, happened the night before, or what party, or what crap joint we'd been in. But now, man, all they do is speak, because like we don't be together. We don't go to the crap games. We don't be with the hos [whores] and shit together.

OTHER ORDINARY PROPERTY OFFENDERS

Both the uncommitted offenders and the successful offenders are exceptions to the pattern described here. The former are exceptions because their criminal careers rarely progress beyond youthful misconduct, a single criminal act, or a series of criminal acts. The experience of arrest and incarceration has a strong impact on their lives. It serves as a painful, graphic portrayal of the consequences of flirtation with ordinary property crime.

In the interviews the uncommitted offenders—especially square johns—consistently stressed that they felt different or set apart from other inmates during incarceration:

Q: Were you scared before you went to the joint?

A: Of course. Outwardly I wasn't, but inwardly I was. I didn't know what to expect. I think the worst part of everything that I can remember, the worst part was when I stopped in Martinsburg, West Virginia. There was a jail there, and that is when I met the lower part of humanity, in that little . . . jail. These people that they depict in movies now, from *Deliverance* and things like that, you never see again in your life. And you never want to be associated with. . . . When you are dealing with me, you are not dealing with the regular criminal. . . . I knew when I was in that institution that this was not the class of people that I was used to. This was not my class of people. . . . I felt I was better than these people.

This man went on to describe another reaction—shame—which appears repeatedly in the interviews with uncommitted offenders:

> I was with two other prisoners, being transported, and we had to stop somewhere and get gas. And they had us chained with a waist chain and leg shackles and, I guess, handcuffs. And that is the worst part I ever felt, when I got out of that car to go to the restroom, and had eight or nine people looking at me. And the shame of it all.

Such men see little that is romantic or alluring about the lives of their fellow convicts. They need only one serious encounter with the criminal justice apparatus to sketch more starkly for them the undesirable, even painful consequences of involvement in ordinary property crime. As they see it, men who spend time in prison are "losers" and "chumps." An uncommitted offender, confined at age 17 for attempted bank robbery, said,

> I knew I was wrong, and I made up my mind that if I ever got out I wouldn't go back. And I kicked myself a million times for even getting there to start with, 'cause I felt like I was just so different than the rest, than a lot of the rest of them, you know, that just didn't care.

Uncommitted offenders interpret their initial criminal involvement—usually it's their only one—as "stupid" and a "waste of time."

The experiences of successful offenders also are different. Not only do they prosper financially from crime but they assimilate subcultural perspectives that help them cope with adversities such as confinement. Thus, despite experiencing some of the orientational contingencies described here, they remain relatively unaffected. In fact, good thieves and hustlers generally assert that men like themselves are unlikely to modify their criminal behavior in the absence of abrupt, traumatic experiences:

> It takes a shock to turn around a lifetime of one way of living, and training, and everything. But, basically, I doubt, even in those types of people [who change] if you dangle a big enough plum out there, they'll come charging.

In any case, the limited data suggest that, unlike the uncommitted and the unsuccessful, a substantial proportion of successful offenders terminate their criminal behavior involuntarily, in large measure because of the real or imagined infirmities of age.[6] One man told me,

> [O]ver the years that I participated in [crime], while there were a few older [thieves] around, you more or less—seems unkind—but actually what use would you have for them? I don't mean that to be as cruel as it sounds, but here's a guy that's, say, 65 and not too mobile. He can't go up and down walls, and jump off buildings. And his hearing is probably slightly impaired. His eyesight is not too good. Now with all the capable, qualified people that are physically able to go out and do these things, what would you want with him? His knowledge is not that indispensable. In fact, his knowledge is probably outdated.

CONTINGENCIES: TEMPORAL ORDER AND INTERDEPENDENCE

The five contingencies discussed here do not occur in an invariant sequence. They vary in the number that occur, age at which they occur, and their interdependence. Imposition of a rigid temporal and causal order on this process would be arbitrary and, given our present state of knowledge, premature as well.

In some cases, the precise point of occurrence of the separate orientational contingencies cannot be isolated easily. Rather, one or more occur simultaneously, as an "experiential cluster":

> I think I had been up [at the state reformatory]. I just said to myself, "well, shit, this isn't getting me nowhere.".... So I come out and I did get a good job ... and they treated me good, and they trusted me, you know.... And I figured well, these people are good enough to trust me, I'm good enough to play it straight with them.... Then I got married and that more or less helped too.
> Q: How so?
> A: Well, I married a good woman, I guess.

Although the orientational and interpersonal contingencies operate both independently and jointly, each type produces modifications in the nature or reductions in the frequency of criminal behavior. In several cases the two types of contingencies interacted with or followed one another as a dynamic process, with one type setting the stage for occurrence of the other(s). For example, in at least one case establishment of a relationship with a woman stimulated a fundamental recvaluation of the subject's life.

Although the orientational contingencies typically set the stage for the interpersonal one, occasionally the latter occurs independently. It then produces a set of subjective career contingencies that strengthens a man's sense of commitment and his resolve to avoid crime—or at least high-risk crime. Meisenhelder (1977) refers to these secondary subjective contingencies as the "pull of normality." They were of some importance in my subjects' retrospective accounts, especially the feeling of relief over no longer having to fear the police. Several men spontaneously mentioned this as one of the advantages of the "square" life.

> I can go to bed, hey man, I don't have to worry about [the police] kickin' my door down, you know, comin' and gettin' me.

Because I'm not doin' nothin'. And man, I can remember one time, every time I see the police, hey man, I know they was comin' to my house. And sometimes I wasn't wrong. . . . But I don't worry about that now.

Although any combination of the five contingencies usually leads to changes in criminal behavior, the nature of these changes varies. In general, the most abrupt and complete changes seem to result when all five contingencies occur. Nevertheless, we must await further research on aging offenders if we are to acquire a more confident understanding of the differential impacts of *various combinations* of the contingencies discussed here.

PERSPECTIVE CHANGE AS SOCIAL INTERACTION

The foregoing discussion of change in aging offenders has an individualistic bias and tone. It seems to suggest that change is a solitary process. This impression is fostered in part by ex-offenders' descriptions of their journey, which many times are intensely personal. But such an interpretation is erroneous. The process of change for aging offenders, like the process of earlier youthful involvement in crime, is a social and interactional one.

To young men the criminal life appears glamorous, appealing, and deceptively attainable. Some are captivated by its allure. They identify with it and they are confident they can succeed at criminal pursuits. Employing the collective standards of the underworld, they want to succeed on its terms and to be recognized as a success by their criminal peers. Incarcerated, they are surrounded by others of similar age and aspirations. Those who may have doubts about the wisdom of the criminal path are reluctant to acknowledge this openly.

Instead, convicts collectively maintain their resolve and a public faith that these setbacks are only temporary. Invariably, they exaggerate the ease of reversing their criminal fortunes, but they weather their initial penitentiary experience reasonably well. Their dreams remain intact, and may be strengthened.

Young men pay little attention to the few older men they encounter during their initial prison experiences. Occasionally, however, older convicts seek out their younger peers:

> Getting older in the penitentiary, you get a good chance to try to rectify some of the mistakes that you've made, man. You see a young guy, you know he's going down the wrong path. I mean, you sit down and talk to him, especially if they like you.... And you can sit a guy down and tell him, ... go on and tell him how foolish you was, and things. If he make the mistake, then he make it. But, as a person, you've done your duty to him, that young guy. Because I definitely wouldn't want to see any young guy go through life as I have gone through.

Young men ignore these efforts by older convicts to present a less optimistic picture of the criminal life:

> [N]o matter how you try to help some of the younger [inmates], they have this dream, that we may have had at one time in our lifetime, that they're smarter and wiser, and to hell with this old man, and so forth or so on. And when you try to help, to pull their coats to things, they'll tell you to kiss their butt, or so forth and so on.

Surely, the "youngsters" believe, the hard experiences of the older men contain no worthwhile lessons for them. Braly (1976: 118) writes of a man he met in the Nevada State Prison when he was young, and of his reactions to the man:

> Elmer ... had served over thirty years in one institution or another ... and I never doubted, though he still talked

hopefully, he would serve thirty more. I came to know many like Elmer, but the time when I would compare them to myself was still far in the future.

As men fail at crime and begin seriously to take stock of their lives and accomplishments, the collective norms and standards of thieves and hustlers gradually lose their grip on them. They recall the warnings of older inmates, perhaps offered years before, not to be fooled by the assumed ease of committing crime successfully. As they get older, the desire or need to demonstrate competence and success in the world of thieves and hustlers becomes less important to them. As he began to change his perspectives, an English thief writes,

> [I] no longer felt anxious to prove that I was a pro, or that my form was respected and that I was somebody to be looked up to because I knew my way around [Wilson, 1964: 118].

Older men find it less important than previously to show that they can stand up to the prison experience in the subculturally required fashion. Whereas younger men may feel compelled to demonstrate that they can do time "like a man," older men begin to feel released from this obligation:

> When I was younger I felt it was *something* being [in prison]. It really felt like that you finally prove yourself in some way. You finally prove your manhood in some way. Or you finally prove your acceptance by going, doing the bit. But now, that is no longer the case. I ain't tryin' to prove myself to do no bit.

Having reached this point in the process of change, men begin to acknowledge openly their doubts about criminal activities. Although young men often are reluctant to talk openly about their misgivings, aging offenders gradually lose these reservations. Increasingly, they see and acknowledge their arrogant youthful estimates of the prospects for criminal success. They begin to see and appreciate the same changes in convicts who are their contemporaries. Interacting with likeminded others, their changing perspectives are reinforced. They experience a new resolve at least to try an alternative, less risky, way of supporting themselves after release.

NOTES

1. Generations of correctional workers have applied the labels "burn out" or "wear down" to the same phenomenon.
2. Most offender follow-up studies have used juveniles or young adults as their subjects (e.g., Wolfgang et al., 1972). Only a few have followed up offenders into or during adulthood (e.g., McCord and Sanchez, 1983).
3. His parole officer noted in a report that "[he is] a long-time crook, finally settling down (at age 64, no less)."
4. In the parlance of D.C. blacks, committing crimes is known as "throwing bricks at the penitentiary." Committing high-visibility confrontative crimes is known as "throwing the *big* brick."
5. Given the small number of successful offenders I interviewed, I am not as confident about them and the changes they experience with age as I am about unsuccessful offenders. Clearly, however, some good thieves and hustlers change in some of the ways I describe (e.g., Hohimer, 1975). Perhaps they tend to experience these changes later in life than is true of unsuccessful offenders.
6. When *only* orientational maturation occurs, the break with crime tends, at least in the early stages, to be a grudging one.

5

CHANGING PERCEPTUAL CONTROLS AND THE CRIMINAL CALCULUS

Asked to explain why they eventually modified their criminal behavior, the interview subjects pointed to age-related changes in the decision-making process that precedes criminal involvement. In other words, with advancing age they changed their *calculus of ordinary property crime.* Often they contrast their new calculus with the one they employed when they were younger. The latter has been described by a number of delinquency analysts, but the transition to the former has received little attention. Consequently, after a few comments about the calculus of youth, I will move on to a more extended discussion of the calculus of older men.

Calculus and Offenses of Youth

For many juveniles, involvement in delinquency contains a rich variety of motives and subjective meanings. Juveniles "slide into" their initial delinquent acts for a variety of nonrational, often situationally based reasons (Matza, 1964). Although there is little new in this, it is interesting that the interview subjects recalled their earliest crimes this way. A 45-year-old man said,

> I was, like years ago, I was a peeping tom—when I was a kid, you know.... I enjoyed this, you know.... But, anyway, then I got married young, and I had two children. And I had bills, you know. I was a kid and I had a man's responsibility.... Now, what's the best way to make money? With something you know. I had been peeping in windows when I was a kid. So, I knew, you know, like where the windows would open, where the—you understand what I mean? And then [I] broadened my sense. After awhile I started mixing business with pleasure, you know. I would peep and then later come back and, you know, take this or that.

Another man told of his adolescent fascination with automobiles. As a youth, he often roamed through parking lots, admiring the steering wheels of cars. From there it was a short, tentative step to breaking into the cars and stealing their contents.

A great deal of delinquency begins simply as risk-taking behavior and it is only later, with the benefit of accumulated incidents, that it takes on the character and meaning of "crime" (Short and Strodtbeck, 1965). Braly (1976: 11-12) writes,

> I began to steal seriously as a member of a small gang of boys. We backed into it, simply enough, by collecting milk and soda bottles to turn in for the deposits, but, after we had exhausted the vacant lots, empty fields, and town dumps, we began to sneak into garages ... and, having dared garages and survived, we next began to loot back porches, and, finally, breathlessly, we entered someone's kitchen.... Clearly, this was an exercise of real power over the remote adult world and I found it exciting. I liked it.... [A]nd it is only now, some forty years later, that I begin to see how stealing cast me in my first successful role.

Many of the crimes committed by youth are impulsive and poorly planned:

> Q: Did you do a lot of stickups [when you were young]?
>
> A: Oh yeah, you know. . . . [We] stole and shit like that, you know. I didn't give it no thought, no plan, don't know how much money's in it. You know what I mean? Just go in there and say, "we're gonna do it, we're gonna do it." . . . That was it.

The spontaneous pursuit of fun and excitement provides the impetus for some delinquency:

> [When I was a kid] I wasn't a sports enthusiast. I played sports very rarely, but it just wasn't exciting enough. . . . None of [the "normal" adolescent activities] were exciting to me. . . . It's just that we, there was a feeling of participating in something that was daring and dangerous.

To some extent, these collective definitions of misconduct based on expressive vocabularies of motive explain why participants do not always see their activities as criminal. Instead of resulting from a rational decision-making process, they simply "happen," and participants do not appreciate sufficiently the seriousness. A former gang member writes,

> It's funny, but we didn't see ourselves as delinquents or young criminal types. Most of what we were into was fighting other gangs. . . . Sure, we got into other kinds of scrapes sometimes, like vandalism and petty larceny from a street vendor or a store. Most of the time we thought of that kind of stuff as "just playing around"—never as crime [Rettig et al., 1977: 28].

For other youths, participation in delinquency results from the interactional dynamics of peer groups. Some boys experience a situational need to maintain personal status and face with their peers (Short and Strodtbeck, 1965; Jansyn, 1966).

Theft or other acts of delinquency may function to buttress or solidify one's informal ranking within a small group. Youths may occasionally use them as a dramatic, incontrovertible demand for a higher as compared with a lower rank:

> Everybody would look up to me, you know, when I was young. ... And seem like every time they wanted something, they'd come to me and say, "Jack, well, come on and do this," or "help me do this," you know. Fuck it, you know. I had an image I had to live up to, you know. I'd say, "fuck it, man, come on."

Precisely because many of the criminal incidents of youth are responses to group dynamics or moods, they occasionally "break out" in situationally propitious circumstances. An interview subject related an incident of armed robbery that occurred when he was young. His account illustrates some of the foregoing observations about the impetuous nature of juvenile crime:

> [One day] we were just walking up First Street and [one of my companions] said as we were approaching Rhode Island Avenue, "let's go in here and rob this drug store," because [another companion] had a gun. We said, "okay, let's go in here and rob the drug store." Went in there, the soda fountain was filled up ... robbed everybody on the stools. Went back in the post office, stole money orders and stamps and stuff, took the cash box. And we turned our backs on everybody in the store, going out! We didn't know whether the proprietor had a gun or what, but it just so happened that he didn't. But, that's just the atmosphere in which, you know, that took place.

Overall, the interview subjects said that as juveniles and young adults they pursued crime with considerable intensity:

> [W]hen you're young, or when—the people that I've known who are young, it was nothing to go out and break into two or three places a week just *looking* for money.

Similarly, a retired English thief writes that "when you're young you tend to have a go at anything" (Quick, 1967: 142).

While juvenile crime is impetuous and fun, it is also monetarily rewarding. Indeed, to juveniles from economically deprived backgrounds it may appear more rewarding than any legitimate employment available to them. The sums of money garnered from crime may seem princely indeed. Crime opens up for them new worlds of consumption and leisure activities. The 49 imprisoned armed robbers studied by Petersilia et al. reported that often their youthful crimes were motivated by a desire for and pursuit of "high times" (1978: 76).

It seems apparent that many youth become involved in property offenses without having developed an autonomous and rationalized set of criminal motives. Petersilia et al. discovered a similar pattern in their research on imprisoned armed robbers. Their subjects reported using little or no sophistication in planning the offenses they committed in their youth (1978: 60-65). At the same time, they found that the juvenile offenses committed by men in their sample included "expressive elements" far more than was true of the offenses they committed later (1978: 76). (Expressive reasons for committing offenses include such things as hostility, revenge, thrills, or peer influence.)

Juveniles and young adults often have little awareness or appreciation of the legal and personal repercussions of their criminality. This is true especially of their perceptions of time spent in institutions such as training schools and prisons:

> I've seen the time in my life, man, where it might seem foolish, 'cause it seems foolish to me now. When I was in the street, hustling, I'd say, "if I get knocked off and don't get but a nickel"—five years—I said, "hell with it," you know. The only thing would be in my mind, if I got busted could I hang around, try to have my lawyer try to get me some kind of plea or something so I wouldn't get but a nickel. 'Cause I knew I could knock five years out.

A 47-year-old man echoed these remarks, saying that when he was young,

> I don't know, man, I just didn't give a fuck, you know. I was young, simple, man. I didn't care, you know. Shit, doing time, you know, I didn't know what doing time was all about. Doing time to me was nothing, you know.

The net result of these youthful meanings and motives is that the potential repercussions of crime to some extent are blunted. Juveniles neither possess nor bring to bear a precise, consistent metric for assessing the potential consequences of delinquent episodes. They fail to "see" or to calculate seriously their potential losses if apprehended. For many youth, crime is a risk-taking activity in which the risks are only dimly appreciated or calculated.

Calculus and Offenses of Young Adults

This poorly developed youthful calculus is transformed both by the approach of adulthood and by the experience of arrest and adult felony confinement. Young adults develop the ability to see, to appreciate, and to calculate more precisely some of the potential penalties that flow from criminal involvement. Consequently, by late adolescence to their early 20s men begin to develop a keener awareness of the potential costs of criminal behavior. Gradually supplanting the nonrational motives and calculus of youthful offenders is a more clearly articulated understanding of the price they will pay if convicted of crime. In this sense, aging and its associated experiences are accompanied by an increasing rationalization of ordinary property crime.[1]

Their growing rationalization of crime seems to be a turning point for many ordinary property offenders. As Zimring (1981: 880) has noted,

At some point in adolescence or early adult development, most of those who have committed offenses in groups either cease to be offenders or continue to violate the law, but for different reasons and in different configurations. Either of these paths is a significant change from prior behavior.

A substantial majority of the uncommitted apparently drop out of crime at this point.

Paradoxically, others—this includes many unsuccessful and most successful offenders—respond to their developing rationalization of crime with a strengthened belief that they can continue committing crime and make it a lucrative enterprise. This is because they convert their developing rationalization of crime into an increased confidence that they can avoid arrest.

For those who continue at crime, theft increasingly springs from a more autonomous set of motives and meanings. The salience of "expressive elements" gradually declines in the process of criminal decision making. Offenders also develop an awareness of the importance of making crime a rational process. They learn the importance of assessing and committing crimes on the basis of an increasingly narrow and precise metric of potential benefits and costs. In this sense as well, their crimes became more calculating and rational. Money increasingly assumes more importance as a criminal objective. After serving a term in the National Training School, one subject and his friends began robbing gamblers and bootleggers. I asked him,

Q: Did the desire for excitement play any part in those crimes?

A: No, I think the desire for excitement had left. It was, we recognized that it was a dangerous mission then, because we knew that gamblers and bootleggers carried guns and things like that. And it was for, you know, just for the money.

Another man made the same point succinctly, saying that "whatever started me in crime is one thing. But at some point I know that I'm in crime for the money. There's no emotional reason for me being into crime." Finally, an ex-thief has written,

> When I first began stealing I had but a dim realization of its wrong. I accepted it as the thing to do because it was done by the people I was with; besides, it was adventurous and thrilling. Later it became an everyday, cold-blooded business, and while I went about it methodically... I was fully aware of the gravity of my offenses [Black, 1926: 254].

Interestingly, during their young adult years the 49 California armed robbers expressed a new confidence in their ability to avoid arrest for their crimes (Petersilia et al., 1978: 69-70). They reported a marked increase in the sophistication of their criminal planning (although the researchers indicate the men never achieved tactical brilliance) (1978: 60). Pursuit of "high times" declined in importance as a motive for crime (1978: 78) and the need to meet ordinary financial exigencies became more important (1978: 76). Concern about arrest declined substantially (1978: 70).

Young men, however, tend to exaggerate their ability to rationalize their crimes and to commit them successfully:

> Whenever I began to steal it was always with the rationale I wouldn't make the mistakes I had made before.... It didn't occur to me there were literally thousands of ways I could get caught. I was sustained by the confidence nothing truly awful could happen to me [Braly, 1976: 65].

Often they confidently assume there are a finite, manageable number of ways that any particular criminal act can fail (Shover, 1971). Consequently, they analyze past offenses for information they believe will lead to ever more perfect criminal techniques and success. Parker's interview (Parker and Allerton, 1962: 149) with an English thief reveals this reasoning process:

> Q: When you're arrested, what are your reactions at that moment?
>
> A: I think the first thing's annoyance—with myself. How could I be so stupid as to get nicked? What's gone wrong, what have I forgotten, where have I made the mistake?

In most cases, young adult offenders' newly acquired faith in their ability to rationalize theft and thereby make it safer proves to be self-defeating. Few of them are equipped by temperament, intelligence, or social connections to follow through on their plans and dreams. Consequently, subsequent offenses usually only repeat the pattern established in their youthful criminal forays.

Calculus and Offenses of Aging Adults

As men age, fail at crime, and experience the contingencies described in Chapter 4, their rationalization of the criminal calculus changes apace. Now they enter a third and final stage of their criminal careers. Increasingly, they realize that the expected monetary returns from criminal involvement are paltry, both in relative and in absolute terms.

Simultaneously, their estimation of the likelihood of being arrested increases, as do the objective probabilities of arrest (Petersilia et al., 1978: 36-39).

Because of the nature and length of their previous criminal record, they generally assume that they will be sentenced to prison again if convicted of another felony. There is evidence to support this assumption (Petersilia et al., 1978: 39). Also, older men assume that any prison sentence they receive, given the length of their previous criminal record, will be long. Finally, those who experience an interpersonal contingency are increasingly reluctant to risk losing their new-found social ties. For all these reasons, aging men begin to include factors that previously were absent from their calculus of potential criminal acts. A 46-year-old former addict said,

> If I go out there and commit a crime—now, I got to think about this: Hey, man, I ain't *got* to get away. See what I'm saying? I have—man, it would be just my luck that I would get busted. Now I done fucked up everything I done tried to work hard for, man, you know, to get my little family together.

Perhaps it is not surprising that they increasingly begin to see that their potential losses, if imprisoned again, will be immense.

In sum, as offenders age, their expectations of the potential outcome of criminal acts changes. Their perception of the odds narrows. Now the perceived risks of criminal behavior loom larger. Note that the Rand Corporation's research on 49 armed robbers found that fear of arrest increases during this age period (Petersilia et al., 1978: 70). Little wonder then that a 56-year-old man said,

> I realized that, even though in crime, even though you might get away, let's say 99 times, the one time eliminates your future. You don't have no future. Regardless of what you have gained, you lost all of that. A rabbit can escape 99 times and it only takes one shot to kill him. So, I was a rabbit.... I want to enjoy life. But I know I can't do it successfully by committing crimes.

This does not mean that men cease *thinking* about crime altogether. Rather, they develop a more complex set of reasons for avoiding it in most situations. However, in more advantageous circumstances, some believe they still are capable of resorting to crime:

Now, I'm not going to tell you that if you put $100,000 on that table and I saw an opportunity, that I felt that I could get away with it, that I wouldn't try to move it. But there's no way, even now, there's no way that I would endanger my freedom for a measley four, five, ten thousand dollars. I make that much a year now, you know. And I see the time that I wasted—well, I figure I wasted four or five years when I was younger.

Q: What do you mean, you "wasted" it?

A: In and out of jail.

Those men who continue to pursue a criminal career change their approach to crime. Most decide to avoid some of the crimes more characteristic of their youth. They shift to offenses that are less confrontative and, therefore, less *visible*. Armed robbery is the prototypical highly visible and highly confrontative offense. Shoplifting or selling marijuana represent the other extreme. An imprisoned man said,

> When I go out, I'm goin' for the "soft" stuff. I'm going to book the numbers, you know... but *hard* crime... I gave that up a long while ago.

Thus, there is evidence that ordinary property offenders, once their fear of arrest and confinement increases, shift to other types of criminal activities. In doing so, they believe that they simultaneously reduce the chances of arrest and, even if arrested, increase the chances of receiving less severe penalties:

> You know, it's funny but there's only a few things that a man goes to the penitentiary for: burglary or robbery or something like that. But how many ways of making money are there that you don't have to revert to robbery or burglary? Thousands. I mean [where you're] between being legit and being crooked. You're skating on thin ice and if that ice breaks it's not going to

break bad. You might get your foot wet, you might get a fine or something. What they're [police, prosecutors, courts] really concerned with are these violent cases, man, these people who are causing these headlines and stuff. . . . If I am going to be a thief I might as well be the one who is skating on that thin ice. And a person who is skating on thin ice is less likely to go to the penitentiary. . . . 'Cause if you get arrested boosting, shoplifting, it is generally a fine. If worse comes to worst, you're going to have to have to do a year in the county jail—in some places, nine months.

I caught one number—that ten years, all them robberies—and then, you know, everything I did then was more like a finesse thing. . . . I'm not gonna stick no pistol in nobody's face, man, you know. I'm not gonna strong arm nobody, you know. I'm not gonna go in nobody's house. You understand what I'm sayin'? I'm not gonna do that.

Q: You figure as long as you don't do those things you won't go to the penitentiary?

A: Hey, you better believe it. You better believe it.

Along with this reduction in the visibility of their offenses, men try to reduce the *frequency* of their crimes. One subject, who still engages occasionally in nonviolent felonies, told me how he had changed:

I done got a little *softer*, you know. I done got, hey man, to the point, you know, where, like I say, I don't steal, I don't hustle, you know. But I don't pass the opportunity if I can get some free money. I'm not gonna pass. . . . I don't hustle, you know. I don't make it a everyday thing. I don't go out *lookin'* for things, you know.

Another man said,

When you're younger, you can . . . steal to pay the rent, you know. Hell, you can go out and steal seven days a week. And sooner [or later] . . . you learn that—to me, it's *exposure time,* you know. You don't want to get "exposed" too much.

Petersilia et al. (1978: 27) found the same pattern. The average monthly offense rates reported by their subjects decreased from 3.28 when they were juveniles to 0.64 in their adult years. After changing their approach to crime, some men do continue to commit crime for several years, but eventually they desist from crime. Only a handful of ordinary property offenders continue their criminal behavior into old age.

For most ordinary property offenders who have been unsuccessful at criminal pursuits, Figure 5.1 depicts the relationships between orientational and interpersonal contingencies and the changing calculus of ordinary property crime.

NEGATIVE CASES

Three aspects of the experiences of successful offenders distinguish them from the other types of offenders. First, the former usually develop an autonomous, rationalized calculus of crime at an earlier age, albeit in the same general fashion discussed here. By their late teens, some successful offenders are engaging in carefully planned crimes primarily for the expected monetary gains. Even some successful thieves, however, never entirely slough off all nonmonetary meanings of and motivations for crime:

> I know a guy who's relatively well connected, if you know what I mean, with the Outfit. [Nevertheless, he would] [g]o on any score! Now he needed money like I need a double hernia. But [he] just loved—don't care if there's any money there or not. "Let's go." [It was] [t]he thrill. I never got any thrills like that myself. . . . The only thrill I got [was] counting the money.

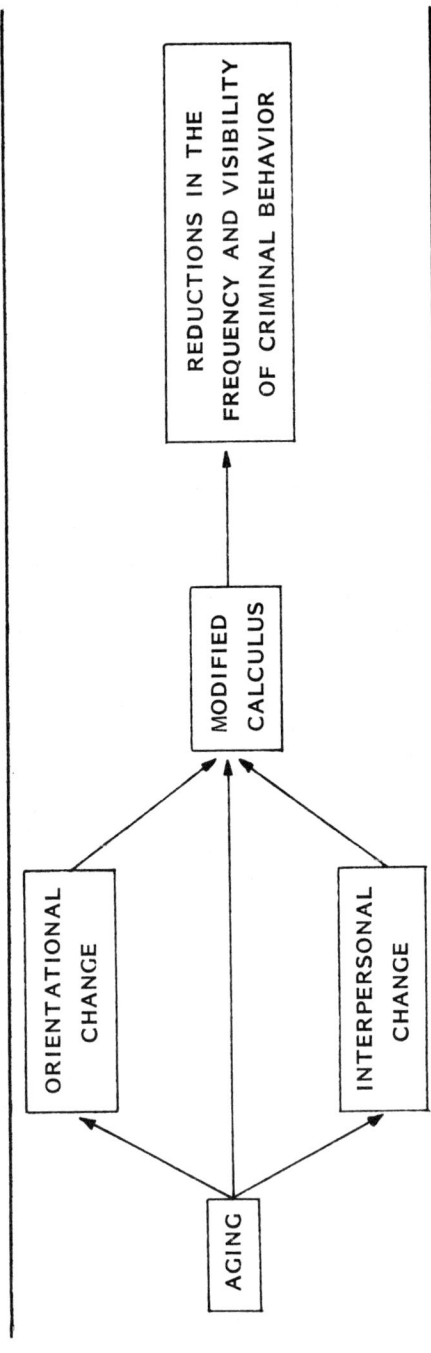

Figure 5.1 Links Among Aging, Changing Perspectives, the Changing Criminal Calculus, and Criminal Behavior

Second, the crimes of successful offenders generally are substantially more rewarding than the crimes committed by other types of offenders. Third, they are more successful than other types of offenders in avoiding incarceration; they spend fewer years in prison. For these reasons, failure at crime does not produce in successful offenders the same impetus to modify their criminal calculus as it does in their unsuccessful peers.

Despite these differences, however, some successful offenders also experience one or more of the contingencies described in Chapter 4. In such circumstances, they respond in ways similar to unsuccessful offenders (Hohimer, 1975). Unlike unsuccessful offenders, however, they sometimes make adjustments in their criminal activities without discontinuing them entirely. They can do so, in part, because their theft activities provide them late career opportunities not available to unsuccessful offenders. For example, because some of them establish extensive social contacts through their work, they can change the nature of their criminal involvement. They are able to shift to other roles in the social organization of theft. Now they eschew the role of *front-line participant* in favor of the role of *background operator* (Mack and Kerner, 1975; Shover, 1983a). Still others manage to save enough money from their working years to retire with a degree of material comfort. One man suggested these two strategies account for most late-life patterns of successful offenders like himself. As he put it, "[T]hey're either sitting in the rocking chair or out finding something soft for somebody else to pick up."

Nevertheless, a substantial percentage of successful offenders apparently continues "going to the well" despite advancing age. An English thief, who already had served several prison sentences, has written,

> I content myself with the dream—the one that all criminals have—that one day I'll get the really big tickle. . . .

That's all I can do now, take my time and wait for the chance to come. I've no intention of going straight, I'm just being more careful, that's all—and I'm getting cagey, I won't take unnecessary risks. It used to be I wanted a fifty-fifty chance, now I want it better than that, somewhere like seventy-five to twenty-five. But sooner or later it'll come, the job will be there, I'll do it, get the big tickle, and then I'll retire.... This is it, this is the dream, the great rock candy mountain that beckons us all [Parker and Allerton, 1962: 189].

This man subsequently was reimprisoned several times (Parker, 1981).

Among the unsuccessful offenders, there are two distinctly different categories of negative cases. Some men simply do not experience the orientational and interpersonal changes described in Chapter 4, and so they fail to modify significantly their calculus of ordinary property crime. In assessing their past criminal behavior these men use almost identical verbalizations: "They [police and the courts] could never get even." They use this description to support their contention that they have avoided arrest and prosecution for so many crimes that, even if they were caught in the future, the ledger books still would show an advantage for them. A man who shoplifts almost daily as a means of support had this to say:

Q: Have you ever thought that you were a good thief, or a good hustler?

A: Yeah, I am. . . .

Q: What makes you think you're a good hustler?

A: 'Cause I *produce*.

Q: Yeah, but you've done a lot of time, too, haven't you?

A: Yeah, but considering, you know, in comparison, I ain't did that much. I think, if they gave me 199 years they couldn't get even. . . . They couldn't get even.

The careers of other unsuccessful offenders are more perplexing. These men, despite their failure at crime and the fact that they experience one or more of the orientational contingencies, react alternately with resignation or despair to the belief that it is too late in life for them to accomplish anything legitimate. In Chapter 6 I discuss their experiences in more detail.

PERCEPTUAL CONTROLS AND DIFFERENTIAL EXPECTATION

Previous research on aging offenders is sparse, but the results are similar to what is reported here (Irwin, 1970; Bull, 1972; Meisenhelder, 1975, 1977; Frazier, 1976; Cusson, 1984). Previous investigators generally concur that aging offenders undergo a number of experiential changes, including development of new commitments and a growing fear of incarceration. These changes cause them to reduce and eventually to terminate their criminal behavior. Results from studies of natural recovery from heroin addiction are consistent as well (Brill, 1972; Waldorf, 1973, 1983; Waldorf and Biernacki, 1979, 1981: Jorquez, 1980).

Although these accumulated research findings lack a secure theoretical home, Frazier (1976) and Meisenhelder (1977) suggest that control theory is a suitable placement. Control theory, they argue, explains why aging men eventually alter their calculus of crime.

Historically, most sociological theories of criminal behavior highlighted the causal importance of social and economic forces that play upon individuals and thereby limit or modify their perceived behavioral options. Gaining new prominence and devotees in the past 15 years, control theory is a clear contrast to this traditional view of crime causation. The hallmark of control theory is the assumption that the probability of criminal behavior increases wherever or whenever *controls* on the individual are weak.

Numerous writers have pointed to or clarified parts of the control process (e.g., Becker, 1955), and they offer somewhat different taxonomies of the controls that ordinarily restrain us. Many, however, include *inner* controls (Reiss, 1951; Reckless, 1961), *relational* controls (Nye, 1958; Hirschi, 1969; Toby, 1974), and *formal* controls (Zimring and Hawkins, 1973; Andenaes, 1974; Gibbs, 1975).

Beyond these areas of agreement, there is considerable diversity in the work of control theorists (Frazier, 1976). There are some nagging problems as well. For example, control theory seemingly suggests that crime simply breaks out whenever controls on the individual are weak.[2] Neither "push" nor "pull" factors are required. By itself, however, weakened controls, like drunkenness (MacAndrew and Edgerton, 1969) and other drug-induced states of altered consciousness (Becker, 1968), do not explain entirely why those in such a condition choose any particular way of behaving. Why should we expect the weakly controlled to engage in crime rather than, say, fall asleep, sing raucously, or become obsessed with their work? How do we explain why they so often choose criminal behavior?

One suggested answer is that weakened controls may increase the interactional influence of delinquent or criminal companions (Hirschi, 1969). In turn, this may increase the attractiveness of criminal behavior and criminal life (Toby, 1957). Therefore, regardless of whether weak controls alone increase the probability of criminal behavior, the same result may occur indirectly via the influence of peers. When they are weakly controlled and associating with criminal peers, the probability exists that individuals will find something alluring about crime. Research has demonstrated the causal importance of these pull factors in the commission of crimes (Hirschi, 1969).

Besides its ambiguity about the influence of pull factors, control theory says little about the social psychology of criminal decision making. Cohen (1965: 8) has labeled this tendency to neglect the criminal decision-making process as the "assumption of discontinuity." He claims that it has led to development of theories "that describe initial states, on the one hand, and outcomes, on the other." The motivational process of criminal behavior is slighted. True, Hirschi (1969: 31-34) correctly notes that several motivational theories are compatible with control theory. But with few exceptions control theorists have neglected the motivational and interpretive processes involved in criminal behavior (Sykes and Matza, 1957; Matza, 1964).

An improved understanding of control processes would benefit from investigations and explication of the social psychology of control and criminal decision-making processes. Just as there are alternative approaches to social psychology, so there are a variety of ways of conceptualizing the criminal decision-making process. The commonsense lessons from deterrence theory and research provide one approach. An improved understanding of deterrence processes begins by highlighting the importance of *perceptual deterrence*. In short, we must enhance our understanding of how individuals *perceive* legal threats.

In like manner, an improved understanding of the social psychology of control could begin with efforts to see it from the actor's point of view. We should strive for an interpretive understanding of the operation of controls and control processes. In doing so, controls can be recast as the *perceived* potential consequences of criminal behavior, both positive and negative. Individuals are most likely to choose crime when perceived or experienced controls are weak and they expect to gain something of value from doing so.[3]

To judge from the literal remarks made by the research subjects, changes in perceptions of a variety of social controls play a major part in the process of desistance from ordinary property crime. Aging men become increasingly aware of the expected advantages and risks of engaging in crime. As they become disenchanted with the criminal life and their criminal companions, the allure of crime diminishes substantially. They begin to weigh more carefully all the variables in the criminal decision-making process.

They attach greater, or different, value to formerly taken-for-granted aspects of life, and to calculate more carefully the potential costs of criminal behavior. In sum, aging ordinary property offenders gradually modify their criminal calculus and *choose* not to engage in crime. Given the passage of sufficient years, most reach the point at which they decide, as one of them put it, that they would "rather be a bum in the *street,* than a millionaire in the *penitentiary.*" This process is most likely to occur when the aging offender has experienced one or more of the contingencies described in Chapter 4.

Of extant criminological theories, Glaser's theory of differential expectation seemingly applies well to the social psychology of control/deterrence. The focus of differential expectation theory is the subject's own analysis and evaluation of various behavior options. The theory "asserts that a person refrains from or commits crime because of his or her expectations as to its consequences" (1980: 138-139). Expectations are determined by

(1) "the person's total conventional and criminal social bonds";
(2) "the person's prior learning experiences that have provided skills, tastes, and ideas conducive to gratification in criminal or in alternative pursuits"; and
(3) "the person's perceptions of needs, opportunities, and risks when interpreting momentary circumstances."

Differential expectation theory builds upon the assumption that individuals choose to engage in behaviors that they believe are most likely to prove rewarding. The metaphor of differential expectation theory easily accommodates what this study has shown to be true: that age contributes to and changes the calculus of ordinary property crime. With advancing age, men increasingly become deterred, not so much because of the nature of external social controls, but primarily because of changes within themselves.[4] These changes in expectations and perceived social controls appear to be more important, ultimately, in deterring criminal behavior than is objective variation in the social control apparatus and process.[5]

NOTES

1. Their experiences are similar to those of some adolescent females after coping with an unplanned pregnancy (Zelnik et al., 1981). Often the result is a heightened rationalization of the process of sexual relations, as evidenced by regular use of contraceptives.

2. Another view of the control process argues that weakened controls may *prepare* an individual for crime, but do not ensure it (Matza, 1964). Weak controls—weakened perhaps by situational social processes or the use of linguistic devices—may *facilitate* a criminal behavioral option (Lemert, 1953; Sykes and Matza, 1957; Briar and Piliavin, 1965).

3. The volume of research on perceptual deterrence has increased modestly in the past two decades (Cook, 1980). Three generalizations summarize the current state of scholarly work in this area. First, because most of the research has utilized samples of high school or college students, there is insufficient age variation to permit an adequate analysis of the age-deterrence relationship. Second, the relationship between age and perceptual deterrence apparently varies by offense (Rowe and Tittle, 1977; Tittle, 1980). Third, investigators have employed survey methods almost exclusively. Qualitative methods would seem to lend themselves well to exploration of perceptual deterrence, but few investigators have used them (Gurley, 1974).

For all these reasons, remarks by Rowe and Tittle (1977: 234) seem both applicable and accurate: "[T]here are complex interactions that contribute to the decline in criminal inclinations as one grows older."

4. It is a mistake to single out and emphasize as some have (Langan and Greenfeld, 1983) the importance of any single component of the process of increasing rationality. The process is a complex whole. These changes produce a new definition and appreciation of those controls. Ironically, the harshness of threatened formal social control measures becomes decreasingly important as the targeted population ages.

5. In constructing crime-control policies we should capitalize on the knowledge that the perspectives of offenders and nonoffenders converge as they get older. From a policymaking standpoint, the challenge is to devise programs that hasten this convergence process. It seems likely that neither rehabilitative programs predicated on a view of the offender as "sick" nor policies intended to cow and hold him at bay offer much promise in this regard.

6

THE CRIMINAL CAREER AND RELATED EXPERIENCES IN RETROSPECT

Until recent years, optimistic claims about the reformative powers of the correctional process were touted as justification for a panoply of correctional policies and programs. For nearly twenty years, the reign of rehabilitation seemed secure. It was a heady time for correction devotees.

Few correctional promoters and publicists are as outspokenly optimistic today. Under the combined onslaught of liberal reformers and conservative politicians they have toned down their public allegiance to the goal of rehabilitation. Political leaders who once empowered correctional managers to reduce crime by reforming offenders have become increasingly tightfisted and retributive in their crime control proposals and policies. In the climate of contemporary debate about corrections they hope for little more than simply to be rid of offenders for a specified, ensured period of time. Sentencing code revisions and other policies designed to accomplish this objective have proliferated.

Some of the men who were interviewed for this research began serving penitentiary time more than 40 years ago, in an era that predates even the ascendant popularity of the rehabilitative ideal. They continued their correctional odyssey during the latter era as well. They received a double dose of correctional nostrums. The prison experiences of others were confined to the heyday of correctional optimism. For both groups I was curious about the enduring effects, if any, of their journey. How do their criminal and correctional experiences look from the vantage point, in some cases, of several decades?

I also was motivated to explore some of these enduring effects as a balance to my—admittedly primary—interest in the process of desistance from crime. Historically, a significant measure of criminological research has been grounded on official, state-promoted assumptions about the overriding importance of crime control. One of the consequences of this is our failure generally to "understand the felon's viewpoint," our "misinterpretation of the felon's acts and responses," and the continuation, perhaps, of "misguided policies" in corrections (Irwin, 1970: 2). As a partial, modest redress of this traditional imbalance in criminological research I explored a range of issues with the research subjects, including retrospective interpretations of their criminal behavior, the relationships between these and the subjects' current lives, and opinions about the treatment they received at the hands of the criminal justice apparatus.

RESTROSPECTIVE ACCOUNTS AND REGRETS

The interview subjects were asked to give retrospective interpretations of their earlier lives, especially the portion that was consumed by crime and imprisonment. This general topic was explored with most of the men, and 25 of them were asked specifically if they have any regrets about their past. Only two men said they have none.

When asked what specifically they regret about their past, a variety of answers were given. The men most frequently cited—it was mentioned by 12 of them—the years they "wasted" or had "thrown away" in crime and in prison before forsaking these pursuits. Given a clear choice, all but a handful said that they would have opted for a more conventional life. Had they seen an alternative path to the kinds of goals we generally interpret as signs of modest success, they would have taken it.

The next most frequently mentioned area of regret was the pain and grief their actions caused significant others. In response to the specific question about regret, 5 men gave responses of this type. A 46-year-old man said he regretted that his mother died before he turned away from serious, felony crime:

> All my life, this is all my mother wanted to see me do, what I'm doing now. But I waited too late to do it. Seriously.... She was, you know, she was raising four kids.... And, hey man, she was struggling. She was trying to raise us, man—working—and she didn't have nobody but herself. And, hey man, she worked hard.

An incarcerated offender writes,

> The worst thing I did, the thing I feel most guilty behind is stealing Mom's life. It's like I stole her youth. Can't nothing change that. I can't give back what's gone.... After all she did for me I turned around and made her life miserable. That's the wrongest thing I've done [Wideman, 1984: 90].

It is not always family members that the ex-offender regrets hurting:

> Q: Did prison have an effect on your life?
> A: I think it had an effect on me. I felt sad that I had let some people down that I think had looked for the basic, good quality in me.

Q: Your folks?

A: Probably my folks. More so some teachers and people like that who had really seen the good qualities. I think I had the ability to do good work. They would always say "you can do this" or "you can do anything you want."

Uncommitted offenders gave this type of response most often, but it was common also among the unsuccessful offenders. Unlike the uncommitted and the unsuccessful offenders, successful offenders offered few spontaneous statements of regret for their earlier lives. They had succeeded at crime and they also had come to accept subcultural justifications of their criminality. Thus, there was less reason for them to evaluate critically their former activities.

Asked to provide retrospective interpretations of their earlier criminal behavior, the subjects gave a variety of responses. Some men look inward and attribute their earlier criminal behavior to personal shortcomings or deficiencies. They *internalize* responsibility for their crimes:

I never would *wait* for nothing. I had to have everything, had to have everything *yesterday*. I didn't want to wait until next year—save some money for a car, or this or that, you know. I wanted it right now. So, I'd go out and steal.

A 44-year-old man said,

[I'm] a damn fool. I'm not dumb, I got a hell of an I.Q., 116. I'm not stupid. Why didn't I make something of myself?

Q: Why do you say you're a "damn fool?"

A: Because when I look back, like I say, with my intelligence I could have been something.... Not a big politician, I mean, just could have been something. I might have made a good living. I could have made it in this world. But I never stuck to nothing long enough to really get it down.... And then I'd get in those weak moments [and commit crimes].

Other men look outside themselves for the locus of their difficulties. They assign primary weight to impersonal forces such as racial oppression, family breakdown, or fate. These men *externalize* responsibility for their crimes:

> I was in [a family] environment that I shouldn't have been in, had no business being in, you know. And the only reason I [became involved in crime] was through child abuse. This is my determination of, you know, what my problems stemmed from. . . . [My father] didn't know anything about raising kids. . . . And since my father's death—and my mother raised all the rest of the kids—none of the other ones ever got in trouble.

Similarly, Robert Timmons, who was introduced in Chapter 2, said,

> You must remember I didn't have no way or means of making no money or anything when I was young. So, consequently, I resorted to crimes. Not that I had the natural tendency to do so. It was conditions that forced me to. I had no other choice. I had worked at jobs. I worked at construction, and all that, but I mean as far as having a regular job and getting a regular salary, no.

The distinction between internal and external attributions is helpful in understanding how aging ex-offenders define their current lives.

THE CURRENT LIFE

Inasmuch as most of the interviewed men have put their crime years behind them, I asked them to characterize their present lives. Again, a variety of answers were given. On one hand, some men deeply regret their past. They believe that it irreparably damaged their prospects for a satisfying life today. On the other hand, others believe that it did little lasting damage in their lives and may, in fact, have been a positive experience.

The Despairing

Seligman (1975) has argued that depressive affect often develops when a person is dissatisfied with his or her present circumstances but feels helpless to change them: in short, when the prospects for something better appear bleak. Depression is most severe when one attributes this helplessness to personal or internal shortcomings. This is an accurate description of those subjects who are the *despairing*. They expressed the most severe regrets about their past exploits and present life. Coupled with an awareness of the pettiness and unrewarding results of crime and realization that it did not pay for them is the belief that this misfortune was their own fault. On top of that, they see little hope of reversing the pattern they have established.

Weighed dispassionately, it is difficult to quarrel with this assessment. In the crudest of ledger systems, time spent in prison is time that is *not* spent on more conventional paths, where one acquires the resources and props of an alternative life. The time spent in prison interferes with—if too many years are spent there, it nearly destroys—one's abilities to meet prevailing socially constructed timetables for most conventional careers, such as work and family. The despairing are fully aware of this fact. They realize acutely that the years devoted to crime, and in prison, have thrown them out of synchronization with the normal timetables for achieving success:

> I can't build nothing, I can't build nothing.... I wants to have a good life, you know, but certain things will always be out of my

reach, you know, because it's been so long. I've been incarcerated so long, you know. . . . I missed 25 years of my life that I could have had some fruit, you know, fruits of life. I missed all that. I missed a lot of opportunities, you know. . . . Life really passed me by because I was in the joint.

Two interview subjects expressed regret because their past exploits have left them with fewer options for family life:

[T]hat's one thing I regret, you know, not having my own family, you know, and things like that. That's one phase in my life, man, that I didn't do when I was ready, you know.
Q: Do you feel that you've lost the opportunity to do that?
A: Yes, really.

Having failed to desist from crime early enough in life to entertain options, in most cases the despairing are dependent on diminished financial and social resources. Some feel like outsiders in the wider world:

I did a whole lot of time, man, for nothin', really. Like, it's so ridiculous, you know. I done throwed my whole life away. . . . And stoppin' and thinkin' about the whole situation, you know, it's almost like watchin' a movie, you know—thinking about how life is.
Q: You feel like you're on the outside of life?
A: Oh man, I'm down there. . . . Lookin' at the Roman empire, I'm down there with the lepers, really, you know.

I asked one of the despairing, "What do you regret about your life, if anything?" He replied,

What I regret is that I didn't get into some kind of occupation, where I could have had some security when I got this old. Like, I have such a little work record, that I couldn't even collect Social

Security. So what am I going to do? I don't have nothing to fall back on.

These men compare themselves with siblings or other contemporaries who pursued more legitimate careers and now have achieved at least a measure of material comfort and also supportive family ties:

> Hey man, I just look at how successful and things that my brothers and sisters have been. And I thought at one time that I was really, you know, the one that was gonna be successful, because I was gettin' the money. . . . Hey man, at one time I thought I was sure enough slick. . . . [But] I think I was stupid, man, because I give up all them years, you know, and I didn't get nothin' man.

I asked another man if he is ashamed of his present circumstances. When he responded yes, I asked him why.

> *Look* at me. I'm 52 years old. I don't have anything. I don't have a car. I don't have a place to stay. Have very few clothes, you know? And I have no job. How in the hell can I be anything but ashamed? I can't run around and bullshit myself like some people, and say, "Oh, I'll have it next week." I know that's bullshit, 'cause I'm too old to have it next week. Like I said, I ain't ever gonna be president. . . . I'm not going to be no success. I'm not going to set the world on fire.

The irony of the contrast between their lives and perspectives today and their dreams of two decades earlier is not lost on the despairing:

> Q: Did you, at one time, think that people who went out on a job every day were just slaves or suckers?
>
> A: Right, "suckers" is right. . . . We used to call them suckers, "those workin' suckers," yeah. . . . "Lunch bucket carriers,"

yeah. But that's what I'd do now, you know, since I've matured a little.... [I]n the joint we called them suckers. But, they were *in the streets* and we was *in jail*!

Another man offered substantially similar comments:

I say, a dude that I went to school with—my age—you know—so he's got his own home out there, you know. He's got a family, he done raised a family. He's got his home, you know. I look at him, you know, [and] say, "goddamn, this old nigger hasn't been nothing but an old square nigger, but this is what he done accomplished." Then I look at myself. Hey, I ain't got a motherfucking thing. So who's the square?

The despairing are a large part of that small group of older men who continue their criminality, and trips to prison, well into middle or even old age. Some of them eventually commit suicide (King, 1972). Others, fully aware of their bleak prospects for making it legitimately at their age and lacking any significant stake in conformity, convert their despair into desperation. In such a mood, even high-risk crime seems to present an acceptable risk. Such a person hopes that the potential criminal rewards will reverse at once his long-established pattern of failure (Camp, 1968). An imprisoned man told me that he is ready to return to robbery if he fails to find a secure niche for himself after release:

A lot of guys here tell me, say "man, why don't you straighten up?" I tell them all the same thing: "Why? *Why*?" If I work every day of my goddamned life from now on I'll never have nothing. Only way I'm going to get what I want is to steal it.... I'll be 47 when I get out of here, and there's no way possible for me to ever get ahead now. It's too late in life. A guy's got to start about 21 or 22 [years of age].... I'm just too old now. I'm not going to have nothing....

Q: What do you see in the future for yourself?

A: In the future, for me personally? If I can get out of here, and make it [working] . . . make good enough money to live off of, I'll make it. But if I don't [I'll] put a gun in my hand again, or a checkbook, or something.

After many years in prison, some despairing men seemingly lose their ability to cope with the routine problems of everyday life—it may have been fragile to begin with—and increasingly feel overwhelmed by them. A parolee has written,

I have been in prison most of my life and its effect on me is that I cannot face problems, not having had any at all inside. Very little things can upset [me] to the point of desperation, things that seem ridiculous to a normal person but huge and impossible to overcome for someone like me, and I get into a panic and try and do something silly [Fletcher, 1972: 132].

When released from prison in mid-life these men ineptly commit crimes which, even were they successful, would yield practically no economic return (Parker, 1963). Apparently, they do not care if they are arrested:

So when I went before the Court . . . and the Judge asked me if I had anything to say, I told him I could not live outside, so would he please send me back to prison for as long as he wished. By so doing he would be helping and not punishing me, as I enjoyed being in prison [Fletcher, 1972: 110].

An instructive example of how far some men are willing to carry this kind of decision process is provided by one of the subjects. Several months after the interview he encountered severe strains in his family relationships. An obese, middle-aged man known to police officials in his home territory, he robbed a bank without making any significant effort to disguise his appearance. Apprehended several hours later, he insisted upon pleading guilty at his arraignment. He told the judge that his only friends are police and correctional officials. He was pleased when the judge sentenced him to 20 years.

Another man, who has a good-paying job, said that he can understand the reasoning of desperate men. He said that in similarly desperate circumstances he too would resort to high-risk robbery:

> If I got to a point where it's either go to an old folks' home or an old soldiers' home—[I'd] figure, hell, if I robbed a bank . . . if I got away I'd get enough money to last me the rest of my life. If I got caught, I'd go to prison and they'd give me better treatment there. . . . They got the best doctors there, and they got the best medical care. . . . What would a fella have to lose, even it he went in and *pretended* to hold up . . . if he had nothing to lose on the outside?[1]

Another member of the interview sample also adopted this strategy. Following his most recent parole, the 65-year-old subject made a halfhearted attempt to rob the same bank he had tried to rob several years earlier. After nearly 40 years in prison he is resigned to it. Similarly, a 62-year-old man expressed a certain ambivalence about leaving prison someday:

> In a way, I'm looking forward to getting out, and another way it don't much matter to me. . . . I know everybody here. . . . I do almost like I want. I go to early chow. [Earlier today] I went down to the law library and used their copying machine. I can do fairly well what I want to do without anybody buggin' me about it, 'cause all the officials know me.

Believing that the outside world has passed them by, such men no longer see any possibility of making it back into the mainstream of life.

The Satisfied

In marked constrast to the despairing are the *satisfied*. In their own eyes, these men have achieved a measure of success, whether legitimately or through crime. They are not nearly as inclined as the despairing to count their earlier years as wasted. In fact, even those who internalize responsibility for their earlier difficulties often claim that the experience of incarceration contained at least some beneficial aspects. Four men said that it was a good thing, perhaps even necessary. They said that otherwise they might have continued committing crimes until they were hurt or someone was killed:

> Let me say this. I will give it the benefit of the doubt. If it hadn't been for the [criminal justice] system and being caught, I could have gotten worse. I will say that.
> Q: Why?
> A: Because the more you do, the more you get away with, the worse it gets.
>
> I look at it [incarceration] as a blessing in disguise. Because if I hadn't been caught the way that I did, who's to say that I wouldn't have went on and did something bigger or worser, and probably been killed. Or got more time. . . . [I]t's just like anything else. When you start to getting away with things, you always think that you're *not* going to get caught, or you're too big to get caught.

In response to the question whether he regretted the years he spent in prison, a 45-year-old man said,

> Well see, the idea sticks out in my mind that it took what happened, it was necessary for what happened to me to get to where I am at now, you know. With the outlook I have. And so, if I regret that—what happened—you understand, then I regret being where I'm at. And that might be an academic thought, but I don't feel that it was a great loss, you know.

The Ambivalent

There was a third, smaller group of subjects, the *ambivalent*. These men are vaguely dissatisfied with their present life circumstances; they feel as though they have fallen short of what they could have accomplished in life. Casting about in their biographies for explanations for this, they single out the experience of crime and imprisonment as a possible culprit. A self-employed man who earns a modest but steady income said that he is not happy with his work or his occupational career:

> I really don't think that I'm matured as well as a person who has never been incarcerated. Because it took three to four years out of my life. I have a tendency to feel that I'm catching up. And you can't catch up with time, I really know that. What's gone is gone.

Another man, now unemployed, expressed a desire to have a steady job. He went on to say,

> I wonder at times what [my life] would have been like if I had never been in jail. And got a job and worked from the time I was younger—what my life would be like today. Where I would be. What position in life I'd have. Would I be better off than I am now or would I be worse off than I am now?

THE PRISON EXPERIENCE

Although they now are middle-aged, the interview subjects recalled the difficulties they encountered as young men in the penitentiary. In this respect, their experiences are like those of most young men. It is difficult for young men to adjust socially and psychologically to the experience of penitentiary time. Put simply, youth complicates the process of doing time. To begin with, young men hear "the siren call of the streets" (Wideman, 1984: 82). Time drags because reverie is devoted to girl friends, spouse, or family.

Youth also are rebellious. Because they have not learned yet how to do time while "going along with the program," they are cited for misconduct more often than older inmates (Goetting, 1983). Recalling his early years in the penitentiary, one man said, you know. I was buckin', you know. . . . I had the ten years, man, but I couldn't adjust, you know, to doing time, especially at the place where I was at, man, you know. There was a lot of prejudice there—hacks, you know. I had some hacks there, man, that couldn't read my name, couldn't spell my name, you know. But I got to say "sir," you know. Speak to them as "sir," and shit like that. And they called me "boy," and stuff like that, you know, and it just fucked me up, you know. And I couldn't cope with it. So I would buck, you understand. I was a "buckin' dude," you know. Call him "sir!" I wouldn't call him shit, you know.[2]

As men age they can do penitentiary time more easily than they did when they were younger. Aging brings with it the experience gained doing time (Goetting, 1983). The older man has developed or learned a variety of habits and mechanisms for managing the physical and mental experience of confinement. He has learned to shut out thoughts of the streets and the people and activities there. Consequently, older inmates often report that penitentiary time passes more quickly than it did when they were younger (Gillespie and Galliher, 1972). I asked a 44-year-old imprisoned subject if he finds it hard doing time.

A: No.

Q: Is it easy for you?

A: I consider it very easy. Time flies.

Q: Is it easier for you to do time today than it was 20 years ago?

A: Oh yeah. Time flies now. I'm old. When I was young, time used to drag. Now the time just flies by. I've done almost five years on this eighteen already. Seems like I just got locked up yesterday.

Having learned how to do time, the older man knows how to avoid many of its pitfalls. Having witnessed the dynamics of prison life, he has learned to anticipate and then to avoid potential trouble (Petersilia and Honig, 1980: 72-74). He has learned not to resist openly his keepers and their policies. To the older inmate, openly rebellious behavior increasingly appears self-defeating.

Although it becomes easier in some ways to do time as men get older, it becomes more difficult for them in other ways. The primary reason is the aging offender's changed conception of time. Men who have begun to see the futility and waste of time spent in prison find it deadening in a special way. Older men value more highly the remaining years of their lives. Aware that life is a finite, diminishing gift, every additional day spent in prison seems especially threatening.

Because of their age, the men I interviewed served their prison time in an era that predates the correctional tumult of more recent times. They served their sentences in the type of institutions Irwin (1980) has dubbed the "Big House" and the "Correctional Institution." In several aspects, American prisons were different places when these men were serving time. This was evident in the interview subjects' accounts of their prison experiences. For example, when they were incarcerated, prison race relations were not as volatile and hostile as they are in the contemporary prison. "Home boy" ties cut across racial lines. Consequently, inmates from D.C. experienced a sense of solidarity with other D.C. inmates, regardless of race.

Their perceptions of the changing nature of institutions add to the difficulties they would expect if they were incarcerated again. Some of them commented on the youthfulness of today's prison population. They see this as the principal source of changes in the prison world in recent years. Largely because of the presence of violent youth, they see contemporary imprisonment as a more dangerous and unpredictable experience than was true when they were going to prison. Former Alcatraz inmates who were still imprisoned when interviewed by Ward and Schmidt said that contemporary prisons are violent, unpredictable—and feared—places. "In prisons like Atlanta, even these men, who are so experienced at doing time, see themselves as potential victims" (Ward and Schmidt, 1981: 67). As one of the interview subjects told me,

> [T]he penitentiaries have changed. There's so much killing in jails now, you know. You don't have to do no hell of a thing to a guy for him to go on and down you, you know. So much killing, you know, like down in Lorton and Atlanta, and different places. And they're taking' guys' lives, man.

Older white men are disturbed by changing race relations in the contemporary penitentiary. These changes have relegated whites to subordinate status in many prisons:

> I heard about this jail down here: 80 percent black. I don't want to go there, man, you know. Although I've did hard time—I did it in Cook County [Chicago] with blacks—these people are getting dangerous, man. Cutting people, and killing people. There's some white haters, you know.

A 58-year-old successful offender said,

> Q: Has the racial composition of prisons made it harder to do time?
>
> A: (Laughs) That's a question that really isn't necessary to ask, is it? ... It's made it a *thousand* times harder. ... Take Atlanta, the last place I was. The ratio had to be like 75 percent black. ... And they seem to get younger and younger, you know. And we're talking about guys in their *early* twenties and, naturally, they don't want anything to do with whitey. ... Goddamn, you wouldn't believe how much harder it is.

Simply being confined with youth can be a problem for older men. Convicts' collective world is dominated by the focal concerns and interests of young men. This proves irritating and aggravating for older inmates. And to men who no longer feel the need to prove their masculinity, much of the convicts' conversation and activity seems superfluous or ridiculous.

Q: Do the main problems of doing time change as you age?

A: They *intensify,* you know. The rhetoric, the environment itself, you know. I mean, who wants to walk around talkin' about fuckin' somebody all day long, or somebody gettin' fucked in the ass and shit? . . . I mean, this kind of shit, you, when you get older you can't relate to that kind of shit.

A 57-year-old man complained about the high level of noise and general disorder in the contemporary prison:

[N]owadays, even the correction officers are dissatisfied. . . . With all the young inmates there, I couldn't hardly survive there. . . . They got a lot of activities that you can participate in, that keep you busy during your off hours. But eventually you have to come back to your bunk. Now everybody got a radio. Everybody playing their radio, different stations! Now how in the world you think I could survive in this circumstances.

Having come to see the shallowness of goals held up for loyalty and pursuit in the prison world, older convicts are less inclined to hustle for what increasingly seem to be petty rewards. Some of the peculiar dynamism of the prison experience is lost in the process. For a variety of reasons, then, many men said that they could not serve penitentiary time today.

THE CORRECTIONAL PROCESS

Reflecting on their earlier years, these men are quick to acknowledge the wrongfulness of their deeds. Still, they believe that they were punished more harshly than contemporary offenders would be.

I deserved what I got, but [the crime] shouldn't have been stressed so much, I guess. Since then, the things that people get away with, the crimes that are perpetuated, the lack of punishment. . . . It does seem a shame. I deserved what I got, but I think the judge should have been a little more lenient, considering.

This reaction was voiced most intensely by uncommitted offenders:

[T]hey was kind of hard on me. I think 2-12 years is a hard sentence for what I did . . . being that I'm a first offender. I mean, I never did this before. . . . But I think I got it hard. I think they made me spend 4 years, out of my life, the first time I done anything like this. And I look at these things today, and these guys out here, for three or four armed robberies, get 2 years. And they're out on parole within a year. That's not justice.

The same reaction was common among other types of offenders as well.

Whatever the opinions of social scientists, black subjects believe there is pervasive racial discrimination in the criminal justice system:

When you be in the penitentiary, all the time you hear this. Like you got the Muslims, they always preachin' this: "Whitey doin' . . ." The things they would say make sense to me. I know this, man: I used to hang with a lot of whiteys, that used as much dope as I did, that was doin' as much wrong. But, man, when you go into jail, you don't see nothing but blackeys in there, you know. . . . And so, man, this must be true.

Irwin has suggested that the prison experiences may leave lasting marks on ex-offenders' perspectives. He says, for example, that they have difficulty in becoming "flag wavers" (1970: 176). This may apply to the men I interviewed. During the period of data collection (1980-1981), the 55 American citizens who were held hostage in Tehran (Iran) were released and returned to the United States. Amid much fanfare, they were given a motorcade parade in Washington, D.C., and were greeted by President Reagan. The interview subjects viewed this entire episode cynically. Few of them were caught up in the public tumult over the return of the hostages. Rather, they expressed the opinion that because the hostages were confined for such a short period of time they were not entitled to so much attention. Three men said that they had spent many years in prison and couldn't understand the reason for all the hoopla. In their view, the hostages were incarcerated for such a short time that they couldn't possibly understand the *real* psychological effects of confinement.

The interview subjects are intimately familiar with involuntary subservience to petty officialdom.. With rare exception, they have come away from this experience with a keen awareness of systematic flaws. Their recalled experiences and appraisals of the system are not inspiring. Most retain a cynical, even jaded, view of the state, its crime control policies, and the ideological justifications if proffers to defend these. Again with rare exception, these men express a bemused contempt for the correctional apparatus and process.

To be sure, some of the men see themselves as ordinary conventional citizens, especially the uncommitted offenders. One of them told me,

> I try to protect [my property] the same as those people would back when I was still a criminal. Back then I didn't have a sense of value. Nothing had a value on it, to me. When it belonged to somebody else, it was there to take. I got locks and locks and locks on top of locks in my house, trying to protect myself from the criminal element. I look at the criminal element differently. See, one time I was part of the criminal element. Today I feel, in myself, I'm part of society.

But this man is an exception. His perspective is shared by a minority of the remaining subjects. Instead, many of them seem to be situated near, or perched precariously on, the fence that bounds the world of squares or conventional society.

In research on armed robbers, Cusson (1984) found that his subjects generally were critical of the prison bureaucracies that once confined them. Nonetheless, those men who had given up crime said that they had "acquired a good number of assets there." They said that what they had learned in prison proved "useful the day they had decided to go straight" (1984: 8). They believed that they had benefited in some ways from the experience of confinement, but they would not credit the correctional process for it.

I discovered much the same thing from talking with the subjects of this study. Twenty-two men were asked specifically if there was anything they liked about doing time. Fourteen men responded "nothing." The 8 remaining men pointed to specific ways that they benefited from incarceration. They were proud of the work experience, vocational skills, and the educational work they completed while incarcerated, even if they never used these skills in their later lives. A man who served several prison sentences decided during his last sentence to take part in the college training program.

> The education that I did receive in Terre Haute [penitentiary] is benefiting me tremendously.... I went in, made up my mind. I got seven years. What am I gonna do with it? Sit in the cell block and look at the ceiling, or get in something? So I went to studying.... I just made up my mind I was gonna study. I took courses there, I took Gregg shorthand, I took trig there, math, and I went into English.

These educational efforts paid well for the subject. After his parole he secured a well-paid technical position with an industrial firm. He is satisfied with his work. Like him, others are proud of their accomplishments even if they did occur in a penitentiary setting.

Even as they acknowledge some advantages of the prison experience, ex-offenders insist that their successes there cannot be attributed to the correctional system itself. Any successes they experienced while in its clutches are attributed to their own personal qualities, or to the assistance or intervention of other persons. When the others are correctional employees, the subjects are quick to admit this. One man said that he attended school and learned about data processing during his two correctional stints. He benefited from these experiences, and also from his contacts with the institutional psychiatrist:

> Q: What did you like about prison, or doing time?
>
> A: Well, there wasn't anything I recall that I liked about it. But I got a decent education—I'll say that—that I couldn't have got in the street. But my time wasn't wasted completely. I got a decent education. And the psychiatrist there, he was one of the guys I'll always respect as long as I live, because he made me feel that I was somebody, before Dr. King or Jesse Jackson or the rest of them. He taught me that you are somebody. He gave me a little saying that I'll never forget: "Act the way you like to be, so you'll be the way you act." I've always kept that philosophy. And this guy, he was just a genuine good guy.

This is typical of the men. They have little good to say about the correctional apparatus, but they remember and credit individual employees who treated them with honesty, dignity, or "like a man."

CRIME PARTNERS AND ACQUAINTANCES

As years pass and the prison experience recedes temporally, many men derive enjoyment from chance encounters with others who accompanied them on some part of their journey. Like military buddies—an analogy that several subjects drew spontaneously—these encounters provide an opportunity to relive some of their earlier experiences and to catch up on what has happened to mutual acquaintances. One man said that two of his fellow employees also have criminal records:

> There's some fellas that work [where I work] that was in Atlanta [penitentiary] that I can talk to.... They met me there, and I can talk to them. Every now and then I meet them and we start talking about old times.

Asked if he liked to talk about the time he spent in prison, a 57-year-old man replied,

> Sure, certainly. If you meet a friend that you met back, like you were in the Army, you met an old Army friend. What would you talk about? You'd ask "how is your, how things been?" And you'd say "remember when..." You gonna always revert back to then, ain't you? ... Yes, I enjoy talking to my ex-inmates because we can talk. We can talk about things, and wonder "where is, where is Willie?" Or "where is Joe Blow? You ever heard from him?"

Joking and the retelling of humorous incidents are the order of the day in these encounters:

> Q: [Let] me ask you, Mr.____, do you ever think about that ten years?
>
> A: Oh yeah. I run across people who be reminiscin', talk about what happened. We try to look at what was happenin' then with some humor, you know.... We talk about the ridiculous things that went on, the way people were, the way we were treated, you understand.
>
> Q: Being in the joint?
>
> A: Yeah. The routine that went on there, and the outrageous things that other people did, and so forth and so on, that wasn't so humorous *then,* but in retrospect we can say, "man that was crazy," you know.

Incidents and comments that recall the foolish and dangerous generally are avoided:

> Q: Do you enjoy, on occasion, talking about old scores, or experiences?
> A: Yeah, if there's any humor in them. Not if there's any degree of danger. You seldom ever talk about that. It's not that you've forgotten that, it just seems the humor, it just seems like everybody wants to laugh more than brood or be [morbid]. . . . I wouldn't bring up once in ten years about fighting a river to get across, or running terror-stricken through some woods at four o'clock in the morning and people shooting and screaming. Or laying down on the ground with cops four feet away looking for you—which happens on rare occasions.

Serious, introspective conversations in which the parties openly or tacitly acknowledge their foolishness also are rare and reserved only for close friends:

> We talk to each other on the telephone from time to time, and really talk about, you know, we say "what the heck was wrong with us then?" We just talk about it, you know. I don't understand. I never will be able to understand what was wrong with us. We sure lost a lot of time getting our act together.

In this later stage of the criminal career, the older ex-offender simultaneously relishes in and derives a certain humor from his shared former experiences. In Irwin's account,

> the criminal life is looked back upon with pleasure and excitement. . . . Furthermore, there is an enduring affinity for ex-convicts, others with the same experiences [1970: 202].

Like fellow travelers who survived a perilous journey, they enjoy talking with old comrades about their youthful exploits. They prefer not to talk about the fools they were for beginning the journey in the first place. Those who eschew entirely or carefully limit such contacts and conversations do so largely because they want to avoid any reminder of their earlier, self-defeating behaviors.

NOTES

1. This man subsequently qualified his statement, saying that it applies primarily to federal institutions. It had been nearly 20 years since his last state confinement and, he acknowledged, "I don't know much about these state places."

2. Just as some age-related conditions make serving time difficult for youth, others function to mitigate its privations. Certainly, two of the more important of these are the age homogeneity of the prison population and the fact that one often encounters friends or acquaintances from the streets or from other institutions in which one has been confined.

Methodological Appendix

I employed a variety of strategies to identify, locate, and contact the interview subjects. At the outset, I decided to use any combination of sampling strategies that seemed likely to ensure a wide range of offender types who presented a variety of characteristics in the later stages of their criminal careers. Consequently, the interview subjects should be regarded as an availability sample. In addition to six imprisoned subjects, I conducted 37 interviews in Washington, D.C., and Baltimore, four in northern Ohio, and three in East Tennessee.

Initially, I identified a pool of potential subjects by listing the names of men who were released from any federal penal institution to either Washington, D.C., or Baltimore during the period 1955-1960. This was accomplished by using files at the U.S. probation offices in these two cities. (I reasoned that these men now would be old enough to justify discussing the later stages of their criminal careers.) Then I consulted available records—primarily telephone directories and driver's license records—to secure current addresses and, where possible, telephone numbers for some of these men. I telephoned those for whom I could secure a number, explained the research to them, and asked for their help. I sent letters to those men for whom I had no telephone number. The letter was worded rather vaguely so that it would not create problems for the addressee if another person happened to read it. The letter asked the addressee to contact me at home.

Eventually, 22 of the men I interviewed were located via this process. Socially, they proved to be among the most stable and conventional of the men I interviewed. Consequently, early in the data collection I determined to use other strategies to identify subjects whose careers had taken a somewhat different turn (e.g., those still engaged in crime or those who for some other reason were leading a less conventional lifestyle). At this point, after originally employing an academic research assistant, I employed a black ex-convict to work with me. He provided me with introductions to a number of hustlers, both active and retired. I then selected those whom I wished to interview—13 men from the total of 50.

In the later stages of data collection I was guided by considerations of theoretical sampling (Glaser and Strauss, 1967; Glaser, 1978). For example, in order to obtain a diversity of respondents, I queried U.S. probation officers in four cities for the names of active or former parolees who possessed some theoretically significant characteristic. One of the men located through this process had a lengthy criminal record in his youth but later maintained a crime-free record for 15 years. This period was broken by his involvement in and subsequent incarceration for a bank burglary. Five respondents were identified and interviewed in this way.

Additionally, I contacted an ex-convict whom I had interviewed as part of an earlier project (Shover, 1973). I interviewed him again and through his assistance I located and interviewed 3 additional men. Finally, I interviewed 6 older men incarcerated in federal penal institutions. (Two of these men seem content to live their remaining days in the penitentiary. Both of them are almost 70 years old—one has spent nearly 40 years in various jails and penitentiaries.)

Excepting the imprisoned men, for whom federal prison regulations prohibit payments, each subject was paid the sum of $50 for the interview. The interviews, all of which were tape recorded and later transcribed, ranged from 30 minutes to more than 6 hours in length; the modal length was approximately 2 hours. A topical guide was used to give some minimal, uniform structure and coverage to the interviews. The guide was revised several times during the course of the study. Of the 50 interviews, I conducted 45. The remainder were conducted by the various research assistants.

At the outset I assumed that it would be necessary to interview the men at a time and place of their choosing. Further, I assumed the men would be reluctant to come to the National Institute of Justice (NIJ) or to the offices of the U.S. probation officers—where I was able to use a spare room to conduct interviews. I realized rather early, however, that this was not the case; although most of them were dependent upon public transportation, they generally were willing to meet me anywhere that was convenient. Consequently, I interviewed the men in a variety of locations. Eleven men were interviewed in their own homes, 17 were interviewed in my office, 10 were interviewed at the U.S. probation offices, 6 were interviewed in prison, and 6 were interviewed in other locations (park bench, automobile, restaurant, public library, place of employment).

Having used an availability sample, the study's external validity is limited (Campbell and Stanley, 1966; Cook and Campbell, 1979). I emphasize, however, that this is a problem shared by all or nearly all research on officially processed offenders, even exemplary studies that have a high degree of internal validity. Given the substantial jurisdictional, bureaucratic, and temporal variation in the way *convicted felons* are produced, it cannot be otherwise. Consequently, although I acknowledge the sample's limitations, few if any studies of offenders are free from similar problems.

Granted that ordinary property offenders change their perspectives and behavior as they get older, a more serious problem with the sample is my inability to separate age, period, and cohort effects (Glenn, 1976; Hastings and Berry, 1979; Greenberg, 1983). Age effects—the focus of the study—are changes produced by the aging process. Period effects are changes associated with the unique period of time in which the men have lived, and cohort effects are changes associated with their membership in a group of people born during a particular time. A variety of materials suggest that the changes reported by the subjects reflect a combination of all three influences. An obvious example is the fact that most of the subjects were reared during the Great Depression, an experience that may have influenced them in ways that differ substantially from the experiences of offenders born in later years. Also, I noted earlier that the subjects spent most of their confinement years in penitentiaries—the Big House and the Correctional Institution (Irwin, 1980)—that have given way in recent years to a different, more conflict-ridden type of institution. Men incarcerated in the contemporary prison may experience a different change process as they get older.

The decision to include in the sample a disproportionate number of men who continued their criminal behavior over a period of nearly two decades introduces another problem. Because of these intentional selection biases (Campbell and Stanley, 1966), I cannot analyze confidently the experiences of men who may have terminated their criminal behavior, for whatever reasons, at younger ages.

When the research project was in the planning stages, friends and colleagues suggested it would be extremely difficult to complete. They believed that I would meet with hostility and a lack of cooperation from the ex-convicts I contacted. Gradually, as a result of their expressed concerns, I too developed doubts about the project's feasibility. However, once I began making contacts with the research subjects, I discovered that such concerns were unfounded. Believing that the research might in some way prevent younger men from repeating their mistakes, many of the subjects happily assisted me. As one man said,

> I looked forward to the interview. I could sit here and talk to you for hours and just tell you my theories, and what other

people have done, 'cause I don't think I'm stupid. And I know what I'm talking about, I've been through it.... I would be glad to help in any way. I think it is very interesting.

The men I interviewed seemed to welcome the opportunity to share their retrospective understandings of their youthful experiences. Nearly all the interviews were relaxed, even pleasant experiences for me. This seemed true for the subjects as well. Impressionistically, more than half of the men— approximately 6 of them expressed this spontaneously— seemed to enjoy the opportunity to talk openly and seriously about past experiences that they were unable to talk about with others in their day-to-day lives. In fact, at the conclusion of their interview, two men said they felt they should pay *me* for the interview:

That's the way I feel, 'cause I feel so much better.

Q: I'm not sure I understand that. Why?

A: I don't know, that's just the way I feel, 'cause you sort of give me the feeling to relax myself. And, like I say, I've seen myself but I never told anyone about the way I feel concerning myself before.

In part for reasons such as this, some of them initially declined the $50 interview payment. Eventually, I persuaded them to accept the payment, explaining that it would create accounting problems for me if they failed to do so.

I encountered other problems in managing the interviews. With extreme naivete I originally assumed that I would pay the men with a personal check drawn on the research grant account at a suburban Bethesda, Maryland, bank. But many of the men lacked the credentials required to cash personal checks, although they usually wanted to convert it to cash as quickly as possible. Until later, when I devised a way to pay them in cash, I accompanied some of them to the bank to vouch for their identity. Not only did this create scheduling problems for me, it also produced some interesting encounters between the subjects and bank employees. (Bethesda is the most affluent D.C. suburb.) I specifically recall a day when I accompanied a skid-row resident and a heroin addict to the bank. As the victim of a mugging two days previously the former's face had been ground into the pavement. His face was marked by several large scabs, and he wore an extremely old and dirty overcoat. The addict appeared equally disheveled and, having recently fixed, was nodding. We evoked much interest and noticeable avoidance behavior as we traipsed into the bank.

Clearly, the process of identifying and locating former offenders can be difficult, time consuming, and tedious. Once located, however, they generally are much more approachable and helpful than our fears would lead us to believe.

There were some exceptions. One man I telephoned greeted my request with a great deal of hostility. Another initially seemed willing and cooperative, although the following day I received an inquiring call from his attorney and was told that the subject was not interested in participating in the project. Four men made but failed to keep interview appointments. Moreover, a few men were extremely nervous during the interview and, although most of them relaxed as it progressed, two or three respondents clearly were relieved when it ended.

By the terms of my agreement with the Federal Bureau of Prisons and the Administrative Office of the U.S. Courts, I secured access to the subjects' correctional records prior to contacting them. By examining these records I was able to select those men whom I believed would be useful respondents. Later, all the men I interviewed were asked to sign both a statement of informed consent and a form granting me access to their correctional records. One subject declined to do so and the records of four other men could not be located. In addition to prison and parole records, I secured a current FBI "rap sheet" for all but two members of the sample.

Because most of the men had been arrested and sentenced in the District of Columbia, the rap sheets were of limited value. Unlike other jurisdictions, which routinely provide complete or nearly complete notational information to the FBI, fingerprint notations from the District of Columbia Department of Corrections routinely omit some items of information useful to researchers. For example, many rap sheets do not show the ultimate disposition of arrests. And whereas other jurisdictions usually enter a separate notation when a person arrives at a penitentiary, D.C. officials do not do so. In fact, rap sheets for men confined in D.C. correctional facilities usually do not show even that they received a prison sentence. I had to rely on the subjects' recall or information contained in other correctional records.

The official records were useful largely because they gave me a more complete picture of each man. They also provided a crude validity check for some materials elicited in the interviews. Although the interviews contained numerous minor factual errors, it seemed to me that nearly all of these were the result of faulty recall. Only two men related materials that, seemingly, were falsified intentionally. One insisted he never had used narcotics, even though his correctional records persuasively contradicted this assertion. Another man claimed to be a decorated Korean combat veteran, although his records indicated that he had failed to report for induction and was a mediocre soldier. The records made no mention of combat awards.

Although they are very uneven in quality, the autobiographies of offenders or ex-offenders provided a third source of data. Given their authors' varied abilities and the varied circumstances in which they were written, the unevenness is not surprising. Many were written with little or no assistance from others (e.g., Black, 1926), whereas other authors benefited from the knowledge and expertise of accomplished writers (e.g., Jackson, 1969; Parker, 1963; Rudensky and Riley, 1970). Some were written at a time when the subject had no intention

TABLE A.1
Characteristics of Interview Subjects

	Unsuccessful Offenders (n = 36)	Total (n = 50)
Percent black	63.9	52.0
Percent who served time as a juvenile	52.6	48.0
Mean ($\bar{X}$) adult felony convictions	3.1	2.7
Mean ($\bar{X}$) years of felony confinement	11.1	9.1
Age when interviewed		
Mean ($\bar{X}$)	51.2	51.0
Median	49.5	52.0
Current *primary* means of financial support		
Full-time employment	11**	18*
Part-time/occasional employment	9	10
Welfare or S.S.I.	3	3
Spouse/family/friends	3	6
Semi-retired/retired	–	2
Crime	4	5
Principal type of crime committed by those known to be engaged in crime		
Index crimes	1**	2*
Other felonies	2	4
Misdemeanors	5	6

*Does not include 6 incarcerated subjects; therefore, n = 44.
**Does not include 6 incarcerated subjects; therefore, n = 30.

of abandoning crime (e.g., Parker and Allerton, 1962). Other authors wrote while in the midst of what they hoped would be a permanent transition to noncriminal life (e.g., Parker, 1967). Still others were written some years after the final break with crime (e.g., Martin, 1952; Jack-Roller and Snodgrass, 1982).

As data, these autobiographies suffer from a variety of shortcomings (Geis, 1982; Kobrin, 1982; Short, 1982). Many contain little that is useful for those intent upon gaining an understanding of age-related changes in offenders' perspectives and behavior. Occasionally, however, one of them offers a rich vein of interpretive insights. For example, one cannot read Braly's *False Starts* (1976) and be unimpressed with his description of the changes wrought by advancing age. Al-

Appendix

though such works are rare, they more than compensate for the more numerous and less revealing life histories.

Using official records and the subjects' reports, Table A.1 contains some limited descriptive data on the sample. As can be seen, the 50 subjects' average age is 50 years. Approximately one-half are black. As adults they averaged 2.7 felony convictions, and spent an average of 9.1 years in jails and prisons. When interviewed, a majority were employed, either full or part time. Crime was the principal source of financial support for only 5 of the 44 unincarcerated subjects, but 6 others also said they still engage in crime occasionally. However, these 11 men who are still engaged in crime generally confine their offenses to rather minor, even petty felonies and misdemeanors.

References

Allen, John
 1977 Assault with a Deadly Weapon (edited by D. H. Kelly and P. Heymann). New York: Pantheon.
Andenaes, Johannes
 1974 Punishment and Deterrence. Ann Arbor: University of Michigan Press.
Becker, Howard S.
 1955 "Marihuana use and social control." Social Problems 3 (July): 35-44.
 1962 "Notes on the concept of commitment." American Journal of Sociology 66 (July): 32-40.
 1963 Outsiders. New York: Free Press.
 1968 "History, culture, and subjective experience: an exploration of the social bases of drug-induced experiences," pp. 272-292 in H. S. Becker et al. (eds.) Institutions and the Person. Chicago: Aldine.
Black, Jack
 1926 You Can't Win. New York: A.L. Burt.
Blumstein, Alfred and Jacqueline Cohen (with Paul Hsieh)
 1982 "The duration of adult criminal careers." Submitted to the National Institute of Justice, June.
Blumstein, A., J. Cohen, and D. Nagin [eds.]
 1978 Deterrence and Incapacitation: Estimating the Effects of Criminal Sanctions on Crime Rates. Washington, DC: National Academy of Sciences.
Booth, Ernest
 1929 Stealing Through Life. New York: Alfred A. Knopf.
Braly, Malcolm
 1976 False Starts. New York: Penguin.
Briar, Scott and Irving Piliavin
 1965 "Delinquency, situational inducements, and commitment to conformity." Social Problems 13 (Summer): 35-45.

Brill, Leon
   1972 The De-Addiction Process. Springfield, IL: Charles C Thomas.
Brown, Waln
   1983 The Other Side of Delinquency. Rutgers, NJ: Rutgers University Press.
Bull, James L.
   1972 "Coming alive: the dynamics of personal recovery." Ph.D. dissertation, University of California, Santa Barbara.
Camp, George M.
   1968 "Nothing to lose: a study of bank robbery in America." Ph.D. dissertation, Yale University.
Campbell, Donald T. and Julian Stanley
   1966 Experimental and Quasi-Experimental Designs for Research. Chicago: Rand McNally.
Chaiken, Jan M. and Marcia R. Chaiken
   1982 Varieties of Criminal Behavior. Santa Monica, CA: Rand Corporation
Chilton, Roland and Adele Spielberger
   1971 "Is delinquency increasing? age structure and the crime rate." Social Forces 49 (March): 487-493.
Clark, Charles L. and Earle Eubank
   1927 Lockstep and Corridor. Cincinnati: University of Cincinnati Press.
Cline, Hugh F.
   1980 "Criminal behavior over the life span," pp. 641-674 in O. G. Brim, Jr., and J. Kagan (eds.) Constancy and Change in Human Development. Cambridge, MA: Harvard University Press.
Cohen, Albert K.
   1965 "The sociology of the deviant act: anomie theory and beyond." American Sociological Review 30 (February): 5-14.
Cook, Philip J.
   1980 "Research in criminal deterrence: laying the groundwork for the second decade," pp. 211-268 in N. Morris and M. Tonry (eds.) Crime and Justice: An Annual Review of Research (Vol. 2). Chicago: University of Chicago Press.
Cook, Thomas D. and Donald T. Campbell
   1979 Quasi-Experimentation: Design and Analysis Issues for Field Settings. Chicago: Rand McNally.
Cusson, Maurice
   1984 "Armed robbery: a short-lived career." Presented at the annual meeting of the American Society of Criminology, Cincinnati.
Edwards, Ed
   1972 Metamorphosis of a Criminal. New York: Hart.

Erickson, R. J., W. J. Crow, L. A. Zurcher, and A. V. Connett
  1973 Paroled but Not Free. New York: Human Sciences Press.
Farrington, David P.
  1979 "Longitudinal research on crime and delinquency," pp. 189-348 in N. Morris and M. Tonry (eds.) Crime and Justice: An Annual Review of Research (Vol. 1). Chicago: University of Chicago Press.
  1983 "Further analysis of a longitudinal survey of crime and delinquency." Submitted to the National Institute of Justice, June.
Federal Bureau of Investigation
  1975 Crime in the United States—1974. Washington, DC: Government Printing Office.
Finestone, Harold
  1967 "Reformation and recidivism among Italian and Polish criminal offenders." American Journal of Sociology 72 (May): 575-588.
Fletcher, John William
  1972 A Menace to Society. London: Paul Elek Books.
Frazier, Charles E.
  1976 Theoretical Approaches to Deviance. Columbus, OH: Charles E. Merrill.
Geis, Gilbert
  1982 "*The Jack-Roller*: the appeal, the person, and the impact," pp. 121-134 in the Jack-Roller and J. Snodgrass, The Jack-Roller at Seventy. Lexington, MA: D.C. Heath.
Gibbs, Jack P.
  1975 Crime, Punishment, and Deterrence. New York: Elsevier.
Gillespie, Michael W. and John F. Galliher
  1972 "Age, anomie, and the inmate's definition of aging in prison: an exploratory study," pp. 465-483 in D. P. Kent et al. (eds.) Research, Planning, and Action for the Elderly. New York: Behavioral Publications.
Glaser, Barney G.
  1978 Theoretical Sensitivity. Mill Valley, CA: Sociology Press.
Glaser, Barney G. and Anselm Strauss
  1967 The Discovery of Grounded Theory. Chicago: Aldine.
Glaser, Daniel
  1956 "Criminality theories and behavioral images." American Journal of Sociology 61 (March): 433-444.
  1964 The Effectiveness of a Prison and Parole System. Indianapolis: Bobbs-Merrill.
  1980 "The interplay of theory, issues, policy, and data," pp. 123-142 in M. Klein and K. Teilmann (eds.) Handbook of Criminal Justice Evaluation. Beverly Hills, CA: Sage.

Glassner, B., M. Ksander, B. Berg, and B. D. Johnson
   1983 "A note on the deterrent effect of juvenile vs. adult jurisdiction." Social Problems 31 (December): 219-221.
Glenn, Norvall D.
   1976 "Cohort analysts' futile quest: statistical attempts to separate age, period and cohort effects." American Sociological Review 41: 900-904.
Glueck, Sheldon and Eleanor Glueck
   1937 Later Criminal Careers. New York: Commonwealth Fund.
Goetting, Ann
   1983 "The elderly in prison: issues and perspectives." Journal of Research in Crime and Delinquency 20 (July): 291-309.
Goffman, Erving
   1961 Asylums. Garden City, NY: Anchor Books.
   1963 Stigma. Englewood Cliffs, NJ: Prentice-Hall.
Greenberg, David
   1977 "Delinquency and the age structure of society." Contemporary Crises 1 (April): 189-223.
   1983 "Age and crime," pp. 30-35 in S. H. Kadish (ed.) Encyclopedia of Crime and Justice. New York: Macmillan.
Greenwood, P. W., J. Petersilia, and F. E. Zimring
   1980 Age, Crime, and Sanctions: The Transition from Juvenile to Adult Court. Santa Monica, CA: Rand Corporation.
Gurley, J. William
   1974 "An analysis of perceptions of the reasons for compliance with criminal laws." Master's thesis, University of Tennessee, Knoxville.
Hapgood, Hutchins
   1903 Autobiography of a Thief. New York: Fox, Duffield.
Hastings, Donald W. and Linda G. Berry [eds.]
   1979 Cohort Analysis. Oxford, OH: Scripps Foundation for Research in Population Problems.
Hirschi, Travis
   1969 Causes of Delinquency. Berkeley: University of California Press.
Hirschi, Travis and Michael Gottfredson
   1983 "Age and the explanation of crime." American Journal of Sociology 89 (November): 552-584.
Hohimer, Frank
   1975 The Home Invaders. Chicago: Chicago Review Books.
Irwin, John
   1970 The Felon. Englewood Cliffs, NJ: Prentice-Hall.
   1980 Prisons in Turmoil. Boston: Little, Brown.
Jack-Roller, The and Jon Snodgrass
   1982 The Jack-Roller at Seventy. Lexington, MA: D.C. Heath.

References

Jackson, Bruce
- 1969 A Thief's Primer. New York: Macmillan.

Jansyn, Leon R., Jr.
- 1966 "Solidarity and delinquency in a street corner group." American Sociological Review 31 (October): 600-614.

Jones, Edward et al.
- 1984 Social Stigma. New York: Freeman.

Jorquez, James S.
- 1980 "The retirement phase of heroin-using careers." Ph.D. dissertation, University of California, Los Angeles.

King, Harry
- 1972 Box Man (as told to and edited by Bill Chambliss). New York: Harper Torchbooks.

Kitchener, H., A. K. Schmidt, and D. Glaser
- 1977 "How persistent is post-prison success?" Federal Probation 41 (March): 9-15.

Kobrin, Solomon
- 1982 "The uses of the life-history document for the development of delinquency theory," pp. 153-172 in the Jack-Roller and J. Snodgrass, The Jack-Roller at Seventy. Lexington, MA: D.C. Heath.

Kuhlen, Raymond G.
- 1968 "Developmental changes in motivation during the adult years," pp. 115-136 in B. L. Neugarten (ed.) Middle Age and Aging: A Reader in Social Psychology. Chicago: University of Chicago Press.

Langan, Patrick A. and Lawrence A. Greenfeld
- 1983 Career Patterns in Crime (Special Report). Washington, DC: Bureau of Justice Statistics.

Larkin, Nancy J. and David J. Greenberg
- 1983 "Age-cohort analysis of arrest rates." Presented at the annual meeting of the American Society of Criminology, Denver.

Lemert, Edwin, M.
- 1951 Social Pathology. New York: McGraw-Hill.
- 1953 "An isolation and closure theory of naive check forgery." Journal of Criminal Law, Criminology and Police Science 44: 296-307.
- 1958 "The behavior of the systematic check forger." Social Problems 6 (Fall): 141-149.

Levinson, Daniel J.
- 1978 The Seasons of a Man's Life. New York: Alfred A. Knopf.

Lohman, J. D., L. E. Ohlin, and D. C. Reitzes
- n.d. "Description of convicted felons as a manpower resource in a national emergency." Illinois Division of Corrections. (mimeo)

MacAndrew, Craig and Robert B. Edgerton
  1969 Drunken Comportment: A Social Explanation. Chicago: Aldine.
Mack, John A. and Hans-Jurgen Kerner
  1975 The Crime Industry. Lexington, MA: D.C. Heath.
Martin, John Bartlow
  1952 My Life in Crime. New York: Harper & Row.
Mattick, Hans W.
  1960 "Parolees in the Army during World War II." Federal Probation. 24 (September): 49-55.
Matza, David
  1964 Delinquency and Drift. New York: John Wiley.
McCall, George J. and J. L. Simmons
  1966 Identities and Interactions. New York: Free Press.
McCord, W. and J. McCord (with I. Zola)
  1969 Origins of Crime. Montclair, NJ: Patterson Smith.
McCord, William and Jose Sanchez
  1983 "The treatment of deviant children: a twenty-five year follow-up study." Crime and Delinquency 29 (April): 238-253.
Meisenhelder, Thomas N.
  1975 "The nonprofessional property offender: a study in phenomenological sociology." Ph.D. dissertation, University of Florida.
  1977 "An exploratory study of exiting from criminal careers." Criminology 15 (November): 319-334.
Moberg, David O.
  1953 "Old age and crime." Journal of Criminal Law, Criminology and Police Science 43 (March-April): 764-776.
Neugarten, Bernice L.
  1968 "Adult personality: toward a psychology of the life cycle," pp. 137-147 in B. L. Neugarten (ed.) Middle Age and Aging: A Reader in Social Psychology. Chicago: University of Chicago Press.
Newman, D., E. S. Newman, and M. L. Gewirtz [eds.]
  1984 Elderly Criminals. Cambridge, MA: Oelgeschlager, Gunn & Hain.
Nye, F. Ivan
  1958 Family Relationships and Delinquent Behavior. New York: John Wiley.
O'Mahoney, Maurice and Dan Wooding
  1978 King Squealer. London: W.H. Allen.
Page, Robert
  1984 Stigma. London: Routledge & Kegan Paul.
Parker, Tony
  1963 The Unknown Citizen. London: Hutchinson.

References

1967 A Man of Good Abilities. London: Hutchinson.
1981 Letter to the Author (July 10).

Parker, Tony and Robert Allerton
1962 The Courage of His Convictions. London: Hutchinson.

Petersilia, Joan and Paul Honig (with the assistance of C. Hubay, Jr.)
1980 The Prison Experience of Career Criminals. Washington, DC: National Institute of Justice.

Petersilia, Joan, P. W. Greenwood, and M. Lavin
1978 Criminal Careers of Habitual Felons. Washington, DC: National Institute of Justice.

Peterson, Mark A. and Harriet B. Braiker
1980 Doing Crime: A Survey of California Prison Inmates. Santa Monica, CA: Rand Corporation.

Pollock, Donald
1976 Call Me a Good Thief. London: Howard Baker.

Quetelet, Lambert A. J.
1969 A Treatise on Man and the Development of His Faculties. Gainesville, FL: Scholar's Facsimiles and Reprints.

Quick, Harry
1967 Villain. London: Jonathan Cape.

Ray, Marsh
1964 "The cycle of abstinence and relapse among heroin addicts," pp. 163-177 in H. S. Becker (ed.) The Other Side. New York: Free Press.

Reckless, Walter C.
1961 "A new theory of delinquency and crime." Federal Probation 25 (December): 42-46.

Reiss, Albert J., Jr.
1951 "Delinquency as the failure of personal and social controls." American Sociological Review 16: 196-207.

Reitzes, Dietrich C.
1955 "The effect of social environment upon former felons." Journal of Criminal Law, Criminology and Police Science 46 (July-August): 226-231.

Rettig, R. P., M. J. Torres, and G. R. Garrett
1977 Manny: A Criminal-Addict's Story. Boston: Houghton Mifflin.

Rowe, Alan R. and Charles R. Tittle
1977 "Life cycle changes and criminal propensity." Sociological Quarterly 18 (Spring): 223-236.

Rudensky, Morris and Don Riley
1970 The Gonif . . . Red Rudensky. Blue Earth, MN: Piper Company.

Sagi, Philip C. and Charles F. Wellford
　1968 "Age composition and patterns of change in criminal statistics." Journal of Criminal Law, Criminology and Police Science 59 (March): 29-36.
Seligman, Martin E. P.
　1975 Helplessness: On Depression, Development, and Death. San Francisco: Freeman.
Sellin, Thorsten
　1958 "Recidivism and maturation." National Probation and Parole Association Journal 4 (July): 241-250.
Short, James F., Jr.
　1982 "Life history, autobiography, and the life cycle," pp. 135-152 in the Jack-Roller and J. Snodgrass, The Jack-Roller at Seventy. Lexington, MA: D.C. Heath.
Short, James F., Jr. and Fred L. Strodtbeck
　1965 Group Process and Gang Delinquency. Chicago: University of Chicago Press.
Shover, Neal
　1971 "Burglary as an occupation." Ph.D. dissertation, University of Illinois, Urbana.
　1973 "The social organization of burglary." Social Problems 20 (Spring): 499-514.
　1983 "Professional crime: major offender," pp. 1263-1271 in S. H. Kadish (ed.) Encyclopedia of Crime and Justice. New York: Macmillan.
Sopher, Sharon
　1978 Up from the Walking Dead (as told by Charles McGregor). Garden City, NY: Doubleday.
Stebbins, Robert A.
　1970 "Career: the subjective approach." Sociological Quarterly 11 (Winter): 32-50.
　1971 Commitment to Deviance. Westport, CT: Greenwood Press.
Studt, Eliot
　1973 Surveillance and Service in Parole. Washington, DC: National Institute of Law Enforcement and Criminal Justice.
Sykes, Gresham M. and David Matza
　1957 "Techniques of neutralization: a theory of delinquency." American Sociological Review 22 (December): 664-670.
Tittle, Charles
　1980 Sanctions and Social Deviance. New York: Praeger.
Toby, Jackson
　1957 "Social disorganization and stake in conformity: complementary factors in the predatory behavior of hoodlums." Journal of

Criminal Law, Criminology and Police Science 48 (May-June): 12-17.
1974 "The socialization and control of deviant motivation," pp. 85-100 in D. Glaser (ed.) Handbook of Criminology. Chicago: Rand McNally.

U.S. Department of Justice
1983 Report to the Nation on Crime and Justice: The Data. Washington, DC: Bureau of Justice Statistics.

Waldorf, Dan
1973 Careers in Dope. Englewood Cliffs, NJ: Prentice-Hall.
1983 "Natural recovery from opiate addiction: some social psychological processes of untreated recovery." Journal of Drug Issues.

Waldorf, Dan and Patrick Biernacki
1979 "Natural recovery from heroin addiction: a review of the incidence literature." Journal of Drug Issues 9 (Spring): 281-289.
1981 "The natural recovery from opiate addiction: some preliminary findings." Journal of Drug Issues 11 (Winter): 61-74.

Waller, Irwin
1974 Men Released from Prison. Toronto: University of Toronto Press.

Ward, David A. and Annesley K. Schmidt
1981 "Last-resort prisons for habitual and dangerous offenders: some second thoughts about Alcatraz?" pp. 61-68 in D. A. Ward and K. F. Schoen (eds.) Confinement in Maximum Custody. Lexington, MA: D.C. Heath.

Watson, Frank L. (with Peggy Hoffman)
1976 Been There and Back. Winston-Salem, NC: John F. Blair.

Wideman, John Edgar
1984 Brothers and Keepers. New York: Holt, Rinehart & Winston.

Wilson, Brian
1964 Nor Iron Bars a Cage. London: William Kimber.

Wiseman, Jacqueline P.
1970 Stations of the Lost. Englewood Cliffs, NJ: Prentice-Hall.

Wolfgang, M. E., R. M. Figlio, and T. Sellin
1972 Delinquency in a Birth Cohort. Chicago: University of Chicago Press.

Wooton, Barbara
1959 Social Science and Social Pathology. London: George Allen & Unwin.

Zelnik, M., J. F. Kantner, and K. Ford
1981 Sex and Pregnancy in Adolescence. Beverly Hills, CA: Sage.

Zimring, Franklin E.
   1981 "Kids, groups and crime: some implications of a well-known secret." Journal of Criminal Law and Criminology 72 (Fall): 867-885.

Zimring, Franklin E. and Gordon Hawkins
   1973 Deterrence. Chicago: University of Chicago Press.

Index

actual social identities, 56
age: adjustment to prison, 140-143; changing criminal calculus, 105-126; crime relationship, 20-22, 77; changes of nonoffenders, 85-86
aging: crime, 19-28; changing criminal calculus, 105-117, 124; decreasing criminal involvement, 77-79; expected outcome of crime, 114; interest in employment, 93; maturation, 77; orientational change, 77-92; social relationships, 93; stages of life, 85-86
aging offenders: changes in, 78-104; changing criminal calculus, 105-117; interactional change, 101-103; previous research, 121
Allen, J., 66, 90, 161
Allerton, R., 113, 120, 158, 167
ambivalent, the, 138-139
Andenaes, J., 122, 161
attributions of criminality: external, 131; internal, 130-131

background operator, 119
Becker, H., 27, 55, 96, 122, 161
Berry, L., 153, 164
Biernacki, P., 78, 121, 169
Black, J., 20, 112, 157, 161
Blumstein, A., 22, 161
Booth, E., 20, 161
Braiker, H., 21, 167
Braly, M., 91, 102, 106, 113, 158, 161
Briar, S., 125, 161
Brill, L., 121, 162
Bull, J., 78, 121, 162

Camp, G., 135, 162
Campbell, D., 153, 154, 162
career: contingencies, 27; conventional, 132; defined, 27; objective, 27; subjective, 27
Chaiken, J., 22, 162
Chaiken, M., 22, 162
Chambliss, B., 165
Chilton, R., 21, 162
Clark, C., 20, 162
Clelland, D., 175
Cline, H., 21, 162
Cohen, A., 123, 162
Cohen, J., 22, 161
cohort effects, 153
conduct stigma, 58
Connett, A., 163
control theory, 121-125; assumptions of, 122; assumption of discontinuity, 123; deterrence theory, 123; formal controls, 122; inner controls, 122; perceptual deterrence, 123; problems with, 122-125; pull factors, 122-123; push factors, 122; relational controls, 122; social psychology of control, 123
Cook, P., 125, 162
Cook, T., 153, 162
correctional process, 127, 143-147; awareness of shortcomings, 144; benefits gained from, 146-147; psychological effects of, 145; racial discrimination, 144
crime: aging adults, 113-116; and aging, 19-28; control, 127-128; ordinary property, 21-23; ratio-

nal process, 111-113; young adults, 110-113; youth, 105-110
criminal calculus: changes with age, 105-126; of successful offenders, 117-119; of unsuccessful offenders, 120-121
criminal careers, 11, 15; contingencies, 80-96, 99-101; later stages of, 113-117; related experiences, 127-150; retrospective accounts of, 128-131
criminal justice process, 90-91; analytic view of, 91; opinions of, 128
Crow, W., 163
current life of research subjects, 131-139; ambivalent, 138-139; despairing, 132-137; satisfied, 138
Cusson, M., 78, 121, 145, 146, 162

despairing, the, 132-137
deterrence theory, 123-125; perceptual, 123
differential expectation theory, 121, 124-125
disclosure, 64-75; third-party, 71-75; voluntary, 64

Edgerton, R., 122, 166
Edwards, E., 20, 163
Erickson, R., 78, 163
Eubank, E., 20, 162
experiential changes, 79; interpersonal, 92-96; orientational, 80-92; successful offenders, 97-99; uncommitted offenders, 97-99

Farrington, D., 13, 21, 163
Figlio, R., 170
Finestone, H., 78, 163
Fletcher, J., 20, 136, 163
Ford, K., 170
formal controls, 122
Frazier, C., 17, 78, 121, 122, 163
front-line participant, 119

Galliher, J., 140, 163
Garrett, G., 167
Geis, G., 158, 163
Gewirtz, M., 166
Gibbs, J., 122, 163
Gillespie, M., 140, 163
Glaser, B., 152, 163
Glaser, D., 14, 24, 28, 78, 124, 163, 164, 165
Glassner, B., 20, 164
Glenn, N., 153, 164
Glueck, E., 20, 77, 78, 164
Glueck, S., 20, 77, 78, 164
Goetting, A., 28, 139, 140, 164
Goffman, E., 27, 56, 58, 164
Gottfredson, M., 20, 164
Greenberg, D., 21, 22, 153, 164, 165
Greenfeld, L., 28, 126, 165
Greenwood, P., 28, 164, 167
Gurley, J., 125, 164

Hapgood, H., 20, 164
Hastings, D., 153, 164
Hawkins, G., 122, 170
Hirschi, T., 20, 122, 123, 164
Hoffman, P., 169
Hohimer, F., 104, 118, 164
Honig, D., 140, 167
Hsieh, P., 161
Hubay, C., 167

Illinois Felon Study, 19
inner controls, 122
interpersonal contingencies, 92-96; interdependence, 99-101; temporal order, 99-101; ties to a line of activity, 95-97; ties to another person, 94
Irwin, J., 25, 26, 78, 121, 128, 141, 145, 149, 154, 164

Jack-Roller, the, 20, 158, 164
Jackson, B., 88, 157, 165
Jansyn, L., 107, 165

Jones, E., 56, 58, 76, 165
Jorquez, J., 121, 165

Kantner, J., 170
Kerner, H., 50, 118, 166
King, H., 20, 90, 135, 165
Kitchener, H., 77, 165
Kobrin, S., 158, 165

labeling theory, 55, 75-76
Langan, P., 28, 126, 165
Larkin, N., 22, 165
Lavin, M., 167
Lemert, E., 23, 56, 125, 165
Levinson, D., 86, 165
Lohman, J., 19, 165
longitudinal studies, 13-14, 20; parole prediction research, 77; official data and interviews, 78; inductive approach, 78-79

MacAndrew, C., 122, 166
Mack, J., 50, 118, 166
Martin, J., 20, 87, 158, 166
Mattick, H., 19, 77, 166
maturation, 77
Matza, D., 106, 123, 125, 166
McCall, G., 57, 166
McCord, J., 78, 166
McCord, W., 78, 104, 166
Meisenhelder, T., 78, 83, 100, 121, 166
Moberg, D., 22, 77, 166

Nagin, D., 161
Neugarten, B., 85, 86, 166
Newman, D., 28, 166
Newman, E., 166
Nye, F., 122, 166

objective career, 27
offender types, 23-26; successful, 25-26, 46-54; uncommitted, 25-26, 29-35; unsuccessful, 25-26, 35-46

Ohlin, L., 165
ordinary property crime, 61; calculus of, 105, 120, 125; defined, 23; desistance from, 124
orientational changes, 77-92
orientational contingencies, 80-92; experiential cluster, 100; interdependence, 99-101; temporal order, 99-101

Page, R., 55, 166
Parker, T., 113, 120, 136, 157, 158, 166, 167
passing contexts, 68
perceptual deterrence, 123
persistent offenders, 70-71
Petersilia, J., 21, 78, 109, 112, 114, 117, 140, 167
Peterson, M., 21, 167
Piliavin, I., 125, 161
Pollock, D., 95, 167
Price, J., 51, 52, 53, 54
prison experiences: age and adjustment, 140-141; changing nature of, 141-142; and youth, 142
pull factors, 122-123
pull of normality, 100
push factors, 122

Quetelet, L., 20, 167
Quick, H., 109, 167

rationalization of crime, 111, 117
Ray, M., 78, 167
Reckless, W., 122, 167
regret, 129-130, 133
Reiss, A., 122, 167
Reitzes, D., 20, 78, 165, 167
relational controls, 122
Rettig, R., 107, 167
Riley, D., 157, 168
Rowe, A., 21, 125, 126, 168
Rudensky, M., 157, 168

Sagi, P., 20, 168
sampling, 152-154
Sanchez, J., 78, 104, 166
satisfied, the, 138
Schmidt, A., 78, 141, 142, 165, 169
secondary deviation, 56
self-report studies, 21
Seligman, M., 132, 168
Sellin, T., 20, 168, 170
Short, J., 107, 158, 168
Shover, N., 24, 50, 113, 118, 152, 168
Simmons, J., 57, 166
situational role-identities: defined, 57; interactional salience of, 57; negotiation of, 58
Snodgrass, J., 20, 158, 164
social margin, 62
social psychology of control, 123
Sopher, S., 20, 91, 168
Spielberger, A., 21, 162
spreading stigma, 74
stages of life, 86
Stanley, J., 153, 154, 162
Stebbins, R., 27, 78, 168
stigma: and conversational contexts, 64; defined, 55-56; disappearance, 75-76; disclosure, 64; erosion, 60-62; management of, 61-76; passing, 64; situational variation, 76; spreading, 74; temporal variation, 76; types of, 58; voluntary disclosure, 64
Strauss, A., 152, 163
Strodtbeck, F., 107, 168
Studt, E., 74, 168
subjective career, 27
successful offenders: contingencies, 119; criminal calculus, 117-119; defined, 25-26; experiential changes, 98-99; rationalization of crime, 111-117
Sykes, G., 123, 125, 169

theoretical sampling, 152
third-party disclosure, 65, 71-75
ties: to a line of activity, 95-97; to another person, 94
Tittle, C., 21, 125, 126, 168, 169
Toby, J., 122, 169
Torres, M., 167

uncommitted offenders: defined, 25-26; experiential changes, 97-98; regret, 130
unsuccessful offenders: criminal calculus, 120-121; defined, 25-26; regret, 130

virtual social identities, 56
voluntary disclosure, 64

Waldorf, D., 78, 121, 169
Waller, I., 78, 169
Ward, D., 78, 141, 142, 169
Watson, F., 20, 169
Wellford, C., 21, 168
Wideman, J., 129, 139, 170
Wilson, B., 20, 81, 103, 170
Wiseman, J., 62, 170
Wolfgang, M., 104, 170
Wooton, B., 77, 170

Zelnik, M. 125, 170
Zimring, F., 111, 122, 164, 170
Zurcher, L., 163

About the Author

Neal Shover is Professor of Sociology at the University of Tennessee, Knoxville. In addition to his long-standing interest in the social psychology of crime, he is interested in organizational crime, the regulatory process, and the political economy of corrections. His *Constructing a Regulatory Bureaucracy*, coauthored with Donald Clelland and John Lynxwiler, will be published by SUNY-Albany Press in 1986.